WILLIAM
of
SAINT
THIERRY

WILLIAM
of
SAINT
THIERRY

The Way to Divine Union

selected spiritual writings

introduced and edited by
M. Basil Pennington

New City Press
Hyde Park, New York

For the young monks and nuns of our Order
and for young people everywhere
for whom William wrote.

May William of Saint Thierry help them
to realize their richest hopes.

Published in the United States by New City Press
202 Cardinal Rd., Hyde Park, NY 12538
©1998 New City Press

Cover design by Nick Cianfarani

Library of Congress Cataloging-in-Publication Data:
William, of Saint-Thierry, Abbot of Saint-Thierry, ca. 1085-1148?
    [Selections. English. 1998]
    William of Saint Thierry : the way to divine union : selected
spiritual writings / introduced and edited by M. Basil Pennington.
        p.   cm.
    Includes bibliographical references.
    ISBN 1-56548-106-2 (pbk.)
    1. Spiritual life—Catholic Church.   2. Mysticism—Catholic
Church.   3. Mystical union.   4. Catholic Church—Doctrine.
I. Pennington, M. Basil.   II. Title.
BX2349.W55213   1998
248.2'092—dc21   97-52200

Printed in Canada

Contents

Introduction

I would like to introduce you to my friend, William. He is usually known as William of Saint Thierry, after the monastery where he was abbot for some fifteen years. He might just as well have been called William of Signy, for he spent the last thirteen years of his life as a monk of this Cistercian community and did much of his writing there. William is known to us, of course, because of and through his writings.

In a way William was a man who "wore his heart on his sleeve." This was especially true in his letters of friendship, but all his writings are in a way autobiographical. He was a man of rich passion and emotion. But he was also a very deep theologian. And for him theology was not just something to speculate about. It was the very present and effective ground of his spiritual teaching and one of the driving forces of his ever-questing life. William of Saint Thierry is a story told by God to invite us and guide us along the spiritual journey.

The fact is, though, that we know very little of the beginnings of his story. Where and when he was born, his family — apart from his brother Simon who like William became a monk and an abbot — where he studied, we do not know. Scholars have made all sorts of conjectures and argued long to support them. His significant spiritual journey begins probably in 1119 (not that the years before were not important foundations and contributing factors to this), when he accompanied his abbot on a visit to Bernard of Clairvaux.

This visit was one of the great moments of grace for William. Twenty-five years later he would still describe it with awe. At the time Bernard was living apart from his community under the direction of a quack doctor—it was a matter of obedience. He was settled in a small shack behind the monastery proper. William tells us, those twenty-five years later, that he approached that hovel as he would the altar of God, so inspired was he by the man who dwelt within. William had heard about contemplation and contemplative union with God. Now he "saw" it, incarnate in a man who was to become the spiritual father of his century. The young monk would have liked to stay there, serving this man of God. But his vows called him back to his own monastery. However, William went home a changed man. He carried something of Clairvaux with him. From now on his whole life would be ordered toward a contemplative union with God.

How much this change in William had to do with it, we do not know, but shortly after his return to his own monastery of Saint Nicaise he was elected abbot of the nearby monastery of Saint Thierry. To this ministry he brought the contemplative ideal. I think we have good reason to say that William's first writings not only express his own initial development under the inspiration of Bernard of Clairvaux but also are the fruit of the conferences he gave his monks.

His writings

First we have his little treatise, *On Contemplating God*. In its opening and closing lines he places this treatise in the context of the demands of his abbatial charge. But it is wholly given to an exploration of the contemplative way or ideal. We hear the questing mind of William the theologian at work here. The keenness of William's theological insight not only had a sure grasp on the centrality of Christ's role in the life of the Christian but saw that our life in Christ is wholly ordered to our being one with him in the inner life of the Trinity. Here the Son is totally to the Father in that embrace of love who is the Holy Spirit. This is "where" the potential of our baptism is fully realized. William speaks of it as *unitas spiritus*, a unity of spirit, our spirit with the Holy Spirit—with the Son Christ we are wholly to the Father in the Holy Spirit. This is where contemplation in its fullness takes place.

The Holy Spirit is the love of God, the love of the Father for the Son and of the Son for the Father. As one source, in one embrace they "breathe" forth the Spirit of Love. Love is the way whereby we enter into this. And so, William's searching mind leads him into an exploration of Christian love, set forth in his treatise, *On the Nature and Dignity of Love*. Though the treatise is relatively short, the treatment is quite complete. It begins with the unenlightened and diverse loves that drive the adolescent about and the struggle to bring these into a harmony with a truly human love for Christ. This is the groundwork for the reception and development of the gift of divine love, the charity that is poured out in our hearts. When this love is illumined through illuminating grace and is affected by the touch of God which draws us to him and centers us upon him, then the Spirit's gift of wisdom can operate in us. We have arrived beyond the maturity of an adult Christian to a

wisdom which William ascribed to "old age"—though he
is quick to say this is not necessarily chronological age but
more a maturing of the spirit.

But who is this person who struggles with adolescent
loves, strives toward mature control and vitality and the
wisdom worthy of the wise old man? It is a person of flesh
and blood, of body and soul. This leads William into a
serious study of the human person. His two-part work, *On
the Nature of the Body and the Soul,* is in some ways a curious
work. It certainly demonstrates William's openness. He was
a man who moved with the times and was not afraid of the
advances of science. His study of the human body, while
some of its tenets cause us to smile today, incorporates what
was then the latest teaching of Arabian scholars. He was a
man up to date and deeply concerned about the human
person and human psychology. This may again be a reflection of the Cistercian spirit already at work in this Benedictine, for all the significant Cistercian Fathers engaged in
studies of the human soul and its psychology. It is the
human person who is the lover, who is divinized, who is
brought into the inner life of the Trinity in experiential
union with God.

It is an interesting phenomenon, found still in our times.
How often young abbots are soon laid low with physical
infirmities that force them to stop and take time out. It is
usually a time of great grace and deepening. Bernard of
Clairvaux, as he himself confessed, did irreparable damage
to his own body in his excessive novitiate zeal. So he was
often enough laid up in the infirmary. William was a few
years into his abbatial service when his own health gave
way. By this time he and Bernard had exchanged a number
of letters and perhaps even visits. They had become intimate friends. This is again a mark of the early Cistercian
saints: Friendship played an important role in their lives.
At the Last Supper, Jesus called us to friendship: "I no

longer call you servants but friends." It is through human friendships that we come to understand existentially the kind of devoted love which the Lord wants from us and which he wants to give us in a complete and indeed wondrous mutuality.

When Bernard heard that his friend was confined to his bed, he sent his blood-brother, who was also the Cellarer or Procurator of Clairvaux, to fetch William and bring him to the infirmary of Clairvaux, where the two friends lay side by side as they recuperated. These lovers passed the hours exploring together that book of passionate love, Solomon's *Song of Songs*. When he returned home, fully restored, William wrote down what he could garner from their conversations and produced what is called today the *Brief Commentary on the Song of Songs*. This short work gives us just a sampling, but it presages the major works to come. It certainly whetted William's appetite, and he spent spare moments in the following years gathering all the fragments he could from the writings of the great Western Fathers, Gregory the Great and Ambrose of Milan, which spoke about the Song of Songs. We are fortunate that these collections, real labors of love, have come down to us today.

The days at Clairvaux in intimate union with Bernard only increased William's desire to remain always with this great and very attractive man of God. We are told that every time Bernard traveled outside his monastery he brought home a large band of men who wanted to do precisely what William wanted to do. But this grace was not to be William's. Bernard forbade it and commanded the Benedictine abbot to labor for the renewal of his own monastery and that of his confreres. However, Bernard did accede to William's request and wrote an *Apologia* in defense of the Cistercian way of life. This was destined to become and remain one of Bernard's most popular works. Before publishing it, Bernard asked William to "censor" it. This was

the beginning of years of literary correspondence and collaboration.

The human person is called to be a lover, a divine lover.
This is obviously something beyond mere human capabil-
ity. This is a thing of grace. And so William now turned his
attention to the mystery of grace. Whether William wrote
his *Exposition on the Epistle to the Romans* first or Bernard first
wrote his treatise *On Grace and Free Will*, which he dedicated
to William, or they were writing together and in some
degree of collaboration, we do not know. But William
certainly gives us a very solid chew in this deeply theological
commentary.

One more piece was needed and then all would be in
place: the sacramental life of the Church. It was now
William's turn to dedicate a work to his friend: *On the
Sacrament of the Altar*. What is interesting in this study is
that William in large part employs here the theological
approach which he was one day to challenge in its exagger-
ated form in the works of Peter Abelard.

As Bernard had directed him, the Abbot of Saint Thierry
did work zealously for the reform not only of his own abbey
but of all the Benedictine abbeys of his province. This
culminated in the convocation at Rheims in 1131 of a first
general chapter of Benedictines of the province, not unlike
the general chapters of the Cistercians. At the chapter many
reforms were enacted which were clearly inspired by the
Cistercian reform. Scholars argue that we can very evidently
see the hand of William in the Acts of the Chapter. With
this work behind him, William felt he was now entitled to
lay down the heavy burden of the abbatial office and
embrace the holy leisure of the Cistercian contemplative
life. But Bernard would still hear none of it. In desperation
and frustration William went ahead on his own. He re-
signed. He could not go to Clairvaux where Bernard blocked
the door. Nor to a monastery directly founded from Clair-

vaux, for Bernard would still exercise a good bit of authority in these. So he went to a nearby monastery that was founded by a monastery which had in its turn been founded by Clairvaux. He went to Signy, which had been founded a few years earlier by a group of monks from Igny. William payed heavily for this rashness as he shares with us in his *Meditations*.

This was the first task William set himself to in his newly acquired leisure. It was a leisure that was increased when his friend Bernard got the general chapter to enact that William should be treated as a visiting abbot (was there a little cattiness in this?), living in the infirmary at Signy and having two lay brothers to care for him. William gathered up his clutter of notes and put them into an orderly collection of meditations. He had a particular purpose in mind for this. They trace rather accurately his own struggle to become a man of prayer. They addressed the vexing questions which plagued him. They brought forth the theological insights that cleared his way. They recounted graphically his inner struggle in responding to a more contemplative way of life. William ever had a special love for young men just setting out on the spiritual journey with all its potential. He wanted to share his journey in the hope of helping them "to learn how to pray." It has repeatedly been my experience: As I have entered into these meditations with William not only do I get more insight into the way of prayer but his great zeal has always re-enkindled my own zeal for pursuing a deeper life of prayer.

With these notes cleared off his desk, William was now able to begin to pursue the promise of the *Brief Commentary* and the collected commentary notes from Saint Gregory and Saint Ambrose. Whether William began his *Exposition on the Song of Songs* first or Bernard began his marvelous collection of *Sermons on the Song of Songs* just before him, the two friends were again working side by side, at least literarily. The *Sermons* had the advantage that they could be produced sporadically; and they were through the rest of Bernard's life. The promise of William's *Exposition* was soon blighted. This spiritual father, who was ever partial to the needs of the young, was sorely concerned. He found that many of the young men arriving at Signy had had their faith undermined by an overdose of rationalism. And the cause of it was the writings and lectures of the then very popular Peter Abelard. William got hold of some of Abelard's works, and his keen theological mind quickly discerned what he considered thirteen serious errors. He sounded the call to his friend Bernard to do something about this monk, who was not living as a monk and was undermining the faith of multitudes by his unbalanced teaching. At the same time he left off his work on the *Exposition* and set to work on a refutation of the errors of Abelard. For the rest he left it to Bernard to carry through the campaign to silence this dangerous voice. For his part William turned his loving concern to the disturbed young men. For them he produced not one book but a trilogy on faith. He describes them himself: "That work is divided into two books, the first of which, because it is straightforward and easy, I entitled *The Mirror of Faith*; the second, because it will be found to contain a summary of the grounds and formulations of faith according to the words and the thought of the Catholic Fathers and is a little more obscure, *The Enigma of Faith*. . . . the *Sentences of Faith*, which I drew principally from the works of St. Augustine (they are indeed strong meat and weighty with meaning); they are more akin to the book I mentioned above, entitled *The Enigma of Faith*."[1]

Whether William ever hoped to get back to continue his *Exposition* we do not know. In fact he did not. Nor do we know what led William to go to spend some time—and how much

---

1. *The Golden Epistle*, The Works of William of Saint Thierry, Cistercian Fathers Series, no. 12 (Spencer, MA: Cistercian Publications) Prov. 8, p. 5.

time—at the recently founded Charterhouse of Mont Dieu, not far from Signy. It may be that he was still looking for more solitude and leisure. Maybe he wanted to escape further involvement in the Abelard controversy. Though I suspect what attracted him was the fact that this new form of monastic life was being attacked in much the same way the Cistercians had been attacked. He went to give solace and support. When he returned home to Signy, he continued to do this. He set his pen to parchment and wrote a long letter to the brethren of Mont Dieu, addressing himself in particular to the novices, the young, ever his primary concern. This remarkable letter which tradition has hailed as *The Golden Epistle* contains a certain defense of the Carthusian way. But it is essentially a crowning summation of William's spiritual teaching. It brings into play the essence of what he taught in all his previous writings, placing it in a vitalizing new context of the three stages of the spiritual journey. Inspired undoubtedly by earlier tradition, it is nonetheless a wholly new paradigm which William employs: the animal—rational—spiritual states; *anima—animus—spiritus.*

This spiritual father's teaching career was at an end. Or was it? His long-standing and intimate friendship with Bernard of Clairvaux was well known. Bernard, ever in poor health, seemed to be at death's door. Bernard's admirers, knowing that a biography of Bernard would be necessary for his canonization, besought William to undertake this task for his friend. William finally agreed, provided it would be kept secret until Bernard passed on. Thus William began what has come to be called the *Vita prima Bernardi*, the *First Life of Bernard*. But it was not Bernard who was to hasten on to pass through the portals to eternal life. Before he had completed half his work in drawing this living icon of all his teaching, William himself was escorted into the heavenly kingdom by the Queen herself on her birthday, September 8, 1148.

Translations

We cannot hope in this slender volume to share all the riches of William's life and literary heritage. My hope is that the chosen sampling will not only shed a very encouraging light upon your journey but will invite you to seek out William's works in order to spend more time at the school of this spiritual master. For this purpose I have added to the volume a rather brief selective bibliography. The translations used here are taken for the most part from *The Works of William of Saint Thierry*, published by Cistercian Publications (Kalamazoo, Michigan) in the Cistercian Fathers Series. However, I have not hesitated to revise them when I felt William's Latin could be better expressed. I am grateful to all the translators and editors of Cistercian Publications who have been working with me these past thirty years to make the extensive corpus of Cistercian patristic writings available in English. The labor is far from finished.

Enjoy William, come to know him as a friend and teacher, and he will give you much sure guidance and encouragement on your way. While he writes as a monk, his spiritual teaching is grounded on and is an expression of the baptismal reality of our divine adoption and oneness with Christ the Son. It is therefore a spirituality for every baptized Christian. Taste and see.

M. Basil Pennington, o.c.s.o

The Way of Contemplation

William had seen them in Bernard, the gracious young abbot in the south: love, joy, peace, patience, kindness, long-suffering — all the fruits of the Spirit described by Paul in his letter to the Galatians. What William knew was this: What he saw was what he wanted. It responded to what was deepest within him. He treasured what he had learned from Abbot Bernard of Clairvaux; he sought to put it in practice. He taught it to his monks, and he shared it more widely through his writing.

What essentially is this contemplation, which so transforms and fulfills a life? How does one enter upon the contemplative way?

William's writings, like those of all the Fathers, are full of scriptural allusions and images. He uses one to describe the first step toward contemplation: Father Abraham at the foot of Mount Moriah, "the mountain . . . where the Lord both sees and is seen." He is ready to ascend for his great encounter with God, his final test, opening the way to his becoming the father of untold multitudes, an immensely fruitful life. "Worries and anxieties, concerns and toils, and all the sufferings involved in our enslaved condition" have to be left behind, says William, "with the ass—I mean my body." "Yearnings, strivings, longings, thoughts and affections, all that is within" have to hasten up the mountain with "the lad — my intellectual faculties." The contemplative way begins with going apart for periods of time, short enough: "For we shall come back and that unfortunately all too soon." The daily worldly cares are left behind for a bit, while the mind and heart turn toward God. Guiding thoughts, the fruit of *lectio divina*, sacred reading and reflection, and the affections they have engendered, give birth to deep, heartfelt desire to see God, for union with him. The desire to see God is paramount, the driving force that sets us on the contemplative way.

One quickly realizes that a certain purity of heart is necessary. Sinful attachments make it impossible to leave behind the concerns of the world. It will, of course, be the contemplative experience itself, the experience of God that will truly purify the heart. This is essentially God's work, as indeed is all that is pleasing to God within us. What then do we do? We stand steadfastly on the rock of faith and wait patiently and longingly for the action of God's illuminating grace.

God's reflection in creation invites us to a certain oblique contemplation. This makes us want even more the actual experience of God himself. William here is brought into a consoling realization: "There are two loves, the love of desire and the love of delight. Desiring love is sometimes rewarded with sight; the reward of sight is delight, and delight earns the perfecting of love." The journey is clearer now. We are actually on the way even as we experience the absence or only the oblique reflections of God, for desiring love is ours. God is at work in us.

And the journey goes on. Indeed, there is always more. For we are called to love as God loves, even loving ourselves for God's sake. Here we have an echo, or is it a leading to Bernard's fourth and highest degree of love. William calls this *unitas spiritus*, unity of spirit, a oneness with God in love brought about by the Holy Spirit: "This is the goal, this is the consummation, this is perfection, this is peace, this is 'the joy of the Lord,' this is joy in the Holy Spirit, this is the 'silence in heaven.'" The whole mission of the Son and Holy Spirit is to heal us and stir up this love in us. Alas, in this life it is fully attained "only on occasion, for the space of half an hour or 'for scarcely half an hour.'" But with the thoughts that remain our attention is able to remain more and more fixed on God, more and more is our life retulant with the fruits of the Spirit.

We find some strong theology in William's little treatise *On Contemplating God*, especially in regard to the Most Holy Trinity. This is necessary for us to understand the full significance of his key concept here, *unitas spiritus*, unity of spirit, in which William precisely places the contemplative experience and its transforming effect in our lives. In baptism we are made one with the Son of God in a oneness that is beyond our ability to conceive or fully understand outside of the beatific experience that lies ahead. At the same time the Holy Spirit is given to us as our spirit, whereby our whole being cries out to God: *Abba*, Father. With the Son we are wholly to the Father in the Holy Spirit. In a word we have been brought into the inner life of the Holy Trinity. Paul has told us that we do not know how to pray but that the Holy Spirit prays within us. This is precisely what William is explaining to us here. When we are willing to leave aside all our ordinary cares and concerns and simply be open to God with all the connatural yearning of our divinized spirit, then God—when and how and as much as he wills, with his illuminating grace—enables us even now while we are still on the way to experience in some little way this actual being to God, to see the face of God.

On Contemplating God

"Come, let us go up to the mountain of the Lord and to the house of the God of Jacob, and he will teach us his ways." Yearnings, strivings, longings, thoughts and affections and all that is within me, come and let us go up to the mountain or place where the Lord both sees and is seen! But worries and anxieties, concerns and toils and all the sufferings involved in my enslaved condition, all of you must stay here with the ass—I mean my body—while I and the lad—my intellectual faculties—hasten up the mountain so that, when we have worshipped, we may come back to you.

For we shall come back and that unfortunately all too soon. Love of truth does indeed lead us far from you, but for the brethren's sake the truth of love forbids us to abandon or reject you. But, though your need thus calls us back, that sweet experience must not be wholly foregone on your account. (1)

Desire for God

"Lord, God of hosts, rescue us; show us your face and we shall be saved." But alas, O Lord, alas! To want to see God when one is unclean in heart is surely quite outrageous, rash and presumptuous and altogether out of order and against the rule of the word of truth and of your wisdom! Yet you are he who is supremely good, goodness itself, the life of the hearts of men and women and the light of their inward eyes. For your goodness' sake then, have mercy on me, Lord, for the beholding of your goodness is of itself my cleansing, my confidence, my holiness. You have your own way, my Lord God, of saying to my soul: "I am your salvation." Wherefore, Rabboni, Master supreme, you who alone can teach me how to see the things that I desire to see, say to your blind beggar: "What shall I do for you?"

And you know, since it happens only by your gift, you know how from the inmost depths of my being, after I have put away from me all striving after worldly honors and delights and pleasures and everything else that can—and often does—arouse in me the lust of the flesh or of the eyes or that stirs up in me a wrong ambition, you know how my heart then says to you: "My face has sought you, your face will I seek. Do not turn your face from me, do not turn away in anger from your servant." So look, O my helper of old and my unwearying defender! I know I am behaving outrageously, but it is the love of your love that makes me do so, as you indeed can see even though I cannot see you. And just as you have given me desire for yourself, if there is anything else in me that pleases you, that also comes from you. And even as your blind one runs toward you, you forgive and reach out your hand to help if he stumbles over any obstacle.

The humanity of Christ

Very well then! Let your voice testify deep down within my soul and spirit, shaking my whole being like a raging storm, while my inward eyes are dazzled by the brightness of your truth, which keeps on telling me: "No one shall see me and live." For I indeed am as yet wholly in my sins. I have not learned yet how to die to myself in order to live to you. And yet it is by your command and by your gift that I stand upon the rock of faith in you, the rock of Christian faith, and in the place where truly you are present. On that rock I take my stand meanwhile, with such patience as I can command, and I embrace and kiss your right hand that covers and protects me. And sometimes, when I gaze with longing, I do see the "back" of him who sees me. I see your Son Christ "passing by" in the abasement of his incarnation.

In my eagerness I approach him and, like the woman with the issue, I am ready to steal the healing for my poor ailing soul by furtively touching the hem of his garment. Like Thomas, that man of desires, I want to see and touch the whole of him and—what is more—to approach the most holy wound in his side, the ark's portal that has been made there. I not only want to put my finger or my hand into it but wholly enter into Jesus' very heart, into the holy of holies, the ark of the covenant, the golden urn, the soul of our humanity that holds within itself the manna of the God head. But then, alas, I am told: "Touch me not!" And I hear that word from the Book of Revelation: "Dogs outside!" Thus and deservedly my conscience harries and chastises me, forcing me to pay the penalty for my presumption and wickedness. Then I return to my rock, the rock that is a refuge for the hedge-hogs that bristle all over with sins. And once again I embrace and kiss your right hand that covers and protects me.

Thus far have I perceived and seen, faintly enough indeed. Yet that slight experience has sufficed to kindle my longing afresh so that I can scarcely contain myself for hoping that one day you will remove your covering hand and offer your illuminating grace. Then at last, dead to myself and alive to you, according to the word of your truth, with unveiled face I shall begin to see your face and by that seeing be united to you. O face, face, happy face that merits thus to be united to you through seeing you! It builds in its heart a tabernacle for the God of Jacob and does everything according to the pattern shown it on the mountain. Here truly and fittingly it sings: "My heart has said to you: 'My face has sought you; your face, Lord, will I seek.'"

As I said, by a gift of your grace, looking at all the nooks and limits of my conscience, I desire only and exclusively to see you so that all the ends of my earth may see the salvation of their God. Thus when I have seen him, I will love him whom to love is to live indeed. For, faint with longing, I say to myself: "Who loves what he does not see? How can anything be lovable which is not in some way visible?"

The divine perfections in creation

But who longs for you, O Lord adorable and lovable, beholds without delay the qualities that make you lovable. From heaven and earth alike and by means of all your creatures these qualities present themselves to me and urge me to attend to them. The more clearly and truly these things declare you and affirm that you are worthy to be loved, the more ardently desirable do they make you appear to me. But alas! This experience is not one to be enjoyed with unmitigated pleasure and delight. Rather it is one of yearnings, strivings and frustration, though not a torment without some sweetness. For just as the offerings I make to you do not suffice to please you perfectly unless I offer you myself along with them, so the contemplation of your manifold perfections, though it does give us a measure of refreshment, does not satisfy us unless we have yourself along with it. Into this contemplation my soul puts all its energies. In the course of it I push my spirit around like a rasping broom. And using those qualities of yours that make you lovable, as hands and feet on which to lift my weight, with all my powers I reach up to you, to you who are love supreme and the sovereign good. But the more I reach up, the more relentlessly am I thrust back and thrown into myself, below myself. So I look at myself and size myself up and pass judgment on myself. And there I am, facing myself, a very troublesome and trying business. . . .

When my inward eyes grow blurred and become dim and blind, I pray you with all speed to open them; not as Adam's fleshly eyes were opened to the beholding of his shame but that I, Lord, may see your glory. Then, forgetting all about my poverty and littleness, my whole self will stand erect and run into your love's embrace, seeing him whom I have loved and loving him whom I have yet to see. In this way, dying to myself, I shall begin to live in you. O may this blessedness of being in you be given to me, for whom the worst thing possible is to be in myself!

But, Lord, make haste! Don't delay! The grace of your wisdom or the wisdom of your grace has its short cuts. For there, where there are not rational arguments or lines of thought to lead one on and upward step by step, up to the torrent of your delight and the full joy of your love—there, I say, we to whom you grant it, we who seek faithfully and persist in knocking, there of a sudden we may often find ourselves arrived already! But, Lord, when something of this joy falls to my lot—and it is all too seldom that it happens —but when it does, Lord, then I cry aloud and shout: "Lord, it is good for us to be here! Let us make here three booths, one for faith and one for hope and one for love." Do I ever know what I am saying when I say: "It is good for us to be here"? But then forthwith I fall to the ground as one dead. And when I look around me I see nothing. I find myself just where I was before, back in my sorrow of heart and affliction of soul. Till when, O Lord, till when? How long must I seek counsel in my soul and be vexed in my heart every day? How long will your Spirit thus come and go in mortals, never remaining with them, blowing where she will? But when the Lord leads back the captives of Sion, then shall we be as those comforted, then will our mouth be filled with joy and our tongue with gladness!

Meanwhile, I have been a foreigner too long. I have dwelt with the inhabitants of Kedar, very much an exile have I been in soul. Yet deep within my heart the truth of your consolation and the consolation of your truth reply: "There are two loves, the love of desire and the love of delight. Desiring love is sometimes rewarded with sight; the reward of sight is delight, and delight earns the perfecting of love."

I thank you, then, who by your grace have deigned to speak to your servant's heart and give at least a partial answer to my anxious questions. I receive and embrace this token of your Spirit and with it joyfully look forward to the fulfillment of your promise of which it is the guarantee. So I desire to love you and I love to desire you and in this way I press forward, hoping to make him my own who had made me his own. That is to say, I hope one day to love you perfectly, you who first loved us, you the love-worthy, you the lovable.

6. But does this perfect love for you, this consummation of beatitude in loving you, ever or anywhere exist, O Lord? Is the soul that thirsts for God as for the fount of life ever so satisfied and so fulfilled that she can say: "It is enough"? No matter who or where the person may be who says: "It is enough!" I feel pretty certain that there is some lack in that one! . . .

Unity of spirit

Surely, when a great grace is given to someone who loves God, it is possible for this love to reach the point of loving neither you nor self for self but you and self for yourself alone. And by that we are refashioned in your image after which you created us. For by the truth of your unique nature and by the very nature of your truth you can love yourself only for yourself. You can love neither angel nor human otherwise than for yourself. Oh, the incalculable blessedness of those that merit so to be acted on by God that through unity of spirit they love in God not just some property of God but God himself and love themselves only in God! Like God, they love and approve in themselves what God must approve and love, that is to say, himself. Or, to put it in another way, they love and approve in themselves that which must be loved by both God the Creator and by his creature. In a word, neither the name of love nor love itself belongs by right to anyone nor is owed to any, save to yourself alone. Oh, you who are true Love, love-worthy Lord, this also is the will of your Son in us, this is his prayer for us to you his Father: "I will that, as you and I are one, so they also may be one in us." This is the goal, this is the consummation, this is perfection, this is peace, this is "the joy of the Lord," this is joy in the Holy Spirit, this is the "silence in heaven."

As long as we are in this life, it is given us to enjoy the ineffable peace of the "silence in heaven" — that is, in the soul of the righteous which is the seat of wisdom—only on occasion, for the space of half an hour or "for scarcely half an hour." But with the thoughts that remain, our attention remains fixed on you as in the observance of a perpetual feast day. However, only in that blessed and eternal life of which it is said, "Enter into the joy of your Lord," will the enjoyment be perfect and perpetual. The bliss then will be proportionately greater in that by that time all the things that now seem to hinder or retard it will have been done away with and the eternity of our love will be secure for ever, our perfection will be inviolable and our bliss such that cannot be corrupted.

The love of God and the sending of the Son

Now how is it we are saved by you, O Lord, from whom salvation comes and whose blessing is upon your people, if it is not in receiving from you the gift of loving you and being loved by you? That, Lord, is why you willed that the Son of your right hand, the man whom you made strong for your own self, should be called Jesus, that is to say, Savior, for he will save his people from their sins. There is no other in whom there is salvation except him who taught us to love himself when he first loved us even to death on the cross. By loving us and holding us so dear he stirred us up to love him who first had loved us to the end. This is the righteousness of the sons and daughters of the human family: "Love me, for I love you." One seldom meets a person who can say: "I love you, *in order that* you may love me!" But, as the servant of your love proclaims and preaches, you who first loved us did this, precisely this. You first loved us so that we might love you. And that was not because you needed to be loved by us, but because we could not be what you created us to be except by loving you. Having then in many ways and on various occasions spoken to the fathers and mothers by the prophets, now in these last days you have spoken to us in the Son, your Word, by whom the heavens and all the power of them were established by the breath of your mouth. For you to speak thus in your Son was an open declaration, a "setting in the sun," as it were, of how much and in what sort of way you loved us, in that you spared not your own Son but delivered him up for all. Yes, and he himself loved us and gave himself for us. This, Lord, is your word to us, this is your all-powerful message: the one who, while all things kept silence (that is, were in the depths of error) came from the royal throne, the stern opponent of error and the gentle apostle of love. And everything he did and everything he said on earth, even the insults, the spitting, the buffeting, the cross and the grave, all that was nothing but yourself speaking in the Son, appealing to us by your love and stirring up our love for you.

Love is not constrained

For you, O God, our soul's Creator, knew that this affection cannot be forced in the souls of the sons and daughters of the human family but has to be evoked. And this is for the obvious reason that there is no freedom where there is compulsion. Where freedom is lacking, so too is righteousness. And you, O righteous Lord, you who wish to save us, you never save or condemn anyone otherwise than justly. You are the author of both our judgment and our cause. Sitting upon your throne and judging righteous judgment, you judge the righteousness that you yourself have made. Thus will every mouth be shut and the whole world be made subject to God when you have pity on those on whom you will have pity and extend mercy to those to whom you will be merciful. We could not with justice have been saved had we not loved you. Nor could we have loved you save by your gift. You willed, therefore, that we should love you. So, Lord, as the apostle of your love tells us and as we ourselves have said before, you "first loved us." You love all your lovers first. . . .

Holy Spirit, the Spirit of adoption

Well, then, how do you love us, if you do not love us with love? But, oh, you who are the One supremely good and ultimate goodness, your love is your goodness: the Holy Spirit proceeding from the Father and the Son! From the

beginning of creation the Spirit has been upon the waters
—on the tossing souls of men and women—offering himself
to all, drawing all to himself. And by breathing into and
upon them, by warding off things harmful and supplying
things useful, he unites God to us and us to God. Your Holy
Spirit who is called Love and Unity and Will of the Father
and the Son dwells in us by grace and implants in us the
charity of God. And through that charity he reconciles God
to us. And thus he unites us to God through the good will
that he breathes into us. And in us this vehement good will
goes by the name of love, by which we love what we ought
to love, namely you. For love is nothing other than a
vehement, well-ordered will.

So, then, love-worthy Lord, you love yourself in yourself
when the Holy Spirit, who is the love of the Father for the
Son and of the Son for the Father, proceeds from the Father
and the Son. And that love is so great that it is unity, and
the unity is such that it is oneness of substance—that is the
Father and the Son are of the same being. And you also love
yourself in us by sending the Spirit of your Son into our
hearts, crying: "*Abba*, Father!" through the sweetness of love
and the vehemence of good intention that you have inspired. This is how you make us love you. Or, rather, this
is how you love yourself in us. We first hoped because we
knew your name, O Lord. We gloried in you as Lord and
loved the name of the Lord in you. But now, through the
grace breathed into us by the Spirit of your adoption, we
have confidence that all that the Father has is ours also. So,
through the grace of adoption, we invoke you now under
the same name as your only Son invokes you by right of
nature. But because all this derives exclusively from you, O
sovereign Father of lights, for whom to love is to do good
and from whom comes every good endowment and every
perfect gift, you, I say, love yourself in us and us in yourself
when we love you through you. We are made one with you

just insofar as we are worthy to love you and—as we said just now—become sharers in the fulfillment of your Son's prayer: "I will that, as you and I are one, so they also may be one in us." For we are your people, Lord, God's people, as your apostle Paul says, making the heathen poet's words the vehicle of good, so that only the savor of good thought should be sensed. We are, I say, God's offspring. We, all of us, are gods and children of the Most High through a kind of spiritual kinship. We claim for ourselves a closer relationship with you, because through the Spirit of adoption your Son does not scorn to be known by the same name as we, and because with and by him, taught by saving precept and schooled by God's ordinance, we make bold to say: "Our Father, who art in heaven."

You, therefore, love us insofar as you make us lovers of yourself. And we love you insofar as we receive your Spirit, who is your love, and let him lay hold of and possess all our secret affections, transmuting them into the perfect purity of your truth and the truth of your purity, into full accord with your love. This union, this adherence, this enjoyment of your sweetness will be such that our Lord, your Son, will call it unity, saying: "That they may be one in us." And so great is the dignity of this unity and so great its glory that he goes on to say, "as you and I are one." Oh, the joy, the glory, the riches, the pride of it! . . .

Prayer asking for the Holy Spirit

Oh, you who are adorable, tremendous, blessed, give him to us! Send forth your Spirit and we shall be made, and you will renew the face of the earth! For it is not in a flood of many waters, in the disturbance and confusion of moods, which are as many in number as they are different in kind, that we shall draw near to God. Lord, that disaster, the punishment of Adam's seed, has gone on long enough! Bring your Spirit on earth. Let the sea draw back, let the wilderness of ancient condemnation draw back, and let the parched earth appear, thirsting for the fount of life! Let the dove come, the Holy Spirit, when the great black bird has been driven out and is hunching over his kill! Let the dove, I say, come with the live branch, proclaiming peace with the branch that speaks of renewal and light! May your holiness and hallowing make us holy, may your unity unite us. Through what is indeed a sort of blood relationship, may we be united to God who is love through the name of love. We shall be made one with him through the power of his name.

The Spirit blows whither he will

But why, Lord, all these words? My wretched soul is naked and cold and benumbed. It longs to warm itself at the fire of your love. I have no garment to put on. To cover my nakedness I am constrained to gather poor rages from anywhere I can and sew them together. Like the wise woman of Sarepta who collected a couple of sticks, I out of my wide wilderness and great emptiness of heart have collected only these few twigs, so that when I do come to the tabernacle of my house I may have a handful of flour and a vessel of oil to eat before I die. Or maybe, Lord, I shall not die as quickly as all that! It may be rather that I shall not die at all but live and declare the works of the Lord.

So I stand in the house of solitude like a lone wild ass, having my dwelling in the salty land. I draw in the breath of my love. I open my mouth in your direction. I breathe in the Spirit. And sometimes, Lord, when I, as if with eyes closed, gasp for you like this, you do put something in my mouth but you do not permit me to know just what it is. A savor I perceive, so sweet, so gracious and so comforting that, if it were fulfilled in me, I should seek nothing more. But when I receive this thing, neither by bodily sight nor by spiritual sense nor by understanding of the mind, do you allow me to discern what it is? When I receive it, I want to keep it and think about it and assess its flavor. But forthwith it is gone. Whatever it was, no doubt I swallowed it down in the hope of eternal life. But I pondered long on its effects on me and in so doing I wanted to transfuse into the veins and marrows of my soul a sort of vital sap. I wanted to be rid of the taste of every other affection and savor this alone for evermore. But it very quickly passed. And when, in seeking or receiving or experiencing this, I try to make my memory retain the more precise impressions of its features or to help my fallible memory I try to write something down, this attempt forces me to recognize that there is here what you say about the Spirit in the gospel: "And you do not know whence he comes nor whither he goes." For I have wanted to commit the particular features of the experience to memory so that I could in a way go back to it and take it to myself again whenever I was so minded, and so submit this power to my will whenever I chose. But every time I attempt this I hear the Lord say to me: "The Spirit blows whither he will." And knowing even in myself that he breathes not when I will but when he himself wills, I find everything devoid of taste and dead. And then I know that it is to you alone, O Fount of life, that I must lift up my eyes that I may see light only in your light.

Toward you, then, Lord, are all things turned—and may my eyes be among them! May every step that my soul takes be toward you, in you and through you. And when my strength, which is nothing, fails, may my very weakness still pant for you! But in the meantime, Lord, how much longer are you going to put me off? How often must my wretched, harassed, gasping soul trail after you? Hide me, I beseech you, in the secret place of your face, away from the troubles of men and women, protect me in your tabernacle from the strife of tongues.

But now the ass is braying again and the lads are clamoring!

A closing prayer

Now, therefore, Lord, in complete faith I worship you. You who are God, the cause of all that is, the wisdom whence the wiseness of every wise person comes, the gift whence every happy person derives happiness. It is you, the only God, whom I honor and bless and adore. It is you whom I love or love to love, whom I long for with all my heart and all my soul and all my strength. Every one of the angels and good spirits who love you, loves me too — me, who also love myself in you; this I know. I also know that everyone who abides in you and can have knowledge of the prayers and thoughts of men and women, hears me in you in whom I also return thanks for their glory. Everyone who has you for treasure helps me in you, and it is not possible for anyone to envy me my share in you. Only the apostate spirit takes pleasure in our wretchedness and counts our benefit his bane. For he has fallen away from the common good and from true happiness and is no longer subject to the truth. Hating the common good, he therefore rejoices in isolation, hugging a joy belonging to himself alone.

You, therefore, God the Father,
by whom as Creator we live,

You, Wisdom of the Father,
by whom we have been made anew
and taught to live wisely,

You, Holy Spirit,

whom and in whom we love
and so live happily and are to live yet more,

You, who are Three in one Substance, the one God,
from whom we are,
by whom we are,
in whom we are,

You, from whom we departed by sinning,
to whom we were made unlike,
but away from whom we have not been allowed
    to perish,

You, the Beginning, to whom we are returning,
the Pattern we are following,
the Grace by which we are reconciled,

You, we worship and bless!
To you be glory for ever! Amen.

Growing Up in Love

Love is the key to union with God and to enjoying him in contemplation. In his treatise on *The Nature and Dignity of Love* William of Saint Thierry explores the origins and the stages of growth of love. Love comes from God, is of God. But first William, ever the Trinitarian theologian and mystic, must speak of our own origin wherein God creates us in his own triune image with memory, reason and will. Each of these powers of the human soul has its vital role to play in the growth of love in us.

In the "youthful" stage of our growth in love it is time to nurture the true natural love-instincts in the human soul while bringing them into service of the love of God. With such solid ground work under way we can begin to walk in the way of that mature or adult love called charity. This is the love that is informed by faith and hope. It is, indeed, a participation in God's own love and expresses itself in our lives in many different ways, which William likens to the various senses of the body.

While charity is a deliberate movement of the will, albeit a gift of grace, it leads to what is wholly a divine gift: the wisdom of "old age." William explores at length the experiential dimensions of this precious gift under the intimate simile of taste. Ultimately our wisdom is Christ, the wisdom of God, who is given to us. Christ's role as our mediator plays a vital part in William's essentially Christian spirituality

We should not fail to note what William says in the concluding paragraph of this treatise. Although he presents these different dimensions of love as developing stages of life, we, in fact, do not grow out of one and leave it behind to grow into another. All should be present in our lives all the time, complementing and supporting one another.

The Nature and Dignity of Love

We want to treat of love insofar as he will assist us whose work itself encourages love. First of all, let us begin this series with the origins of love and then develop our treatise through love's successive stages until we come to a rich old age which is full, not of senile sadness, but of rich mercy. As the various stages of life pass, a child develops into an adolescent, an adolescent into a mature adult and a mature adult into an elder. There are changes in the quality of life, so there are changes in the names of each stage. In the same way as its virtue develops, the will grows into love, love into charity and charity into wisdom.

Concerning the love of which we are treating, we ought to make known the origin from which it takes birth. From this comes its lineage of eminent nobility. . . . Its birthplace is God. There it is born. There it is nourished. There it develops. There love is a citizen, not a stranger but a native. Love is given by God alone. It abides in him, for it is due to no one else but him and for his sake. (3)

The image of God in us

As we discuss love's birth let us remember that when the triune God created us to his own image he formed in us a sort of likeness of the Trinity wherein the image of the Creator-Trinity was to shine out. By this image as a new inhabitant of the world, had we chosen to do so, we might have adhered indissolubly to God our Creator, for like naturally reverts to like. However, led astray, alienated, distracted by the many different varieties of creatures, this lesser, created trinity separated itself from the unity of the supreme Creator-Trinity. When God infused the breath of life, he created his new creature by infusing a spiritual power, an intellectual power which the breath or breathing conveys, and a vital power, an animal power which the name life conveys. At the same time he established in this his "fortress," the power of memory, so that we might always remember the powerfulness and goodness of the Creator. Memory immediately begets reason. Then memory and reason bring forth the will. Memory has that to which we must strive; reason demands that we strive; it is the will that strives. These three, memory, reason and will, are one, yet effectively three. It is just as it is in the supreme Trinity where there is one substance and three persons. In that Trinity the Father is the one who begets, the Son the one begotten and the Holy Spirit the one who proceeds from the two. So reason is begotten from memory and from both memory and reason proceeds the will. That the rational soul created in us may adhere to God, the Father claims the memory for himself, the Son the reason and the Holy Spirit, who proceeds from them both, claims the will which proceeds from the other two. (3)

Love in its youthful stage

This then is the birthplace of the will, its adoption, its dignity, its nobility. When grace anticipates and cooperates, the will begins to cleave by a due assent to the Holy Spirit, who is the love and the will of the Father and the Son. It begins to ardently will what God wills and what memory and reason suggest it should will. By ardent willing, the will becomes love. For love is nothing other than the will ardently set on something good. . . . Without this self-ordering, the will, by the just ordaining of God, rushes headlong into disaster and is overwhelmed in the darkness of confusion. It is buried in a hell of vices, unless help quickly comes to it from grace. If the will truly forsakes this road to hell, it begins its journey upward and, following the grace that leads and nourishes it, it matures into love. With the fortitude of youth, the will begins to move beyond the spirit of fear in which up till then it dwelt like a child afraid of punishment. It moves into the spirit of piety, where it begins to experience new grace and begins to love and reverence God. Of this spirit it is written: Piety is the worship of God. Let the young then put forth their natural strength and power, not of age but of virtue. Let them not dissipate youth's natural incentives. . . . It is a matter of grave disgrace in nature if the corrupt are able to make more progress toward base things than true lovers do toward the good.

The development of love

At this stage it becomes youthful ardor to be conspicuous and the way of religious life to be fervent. . . . We must exercise over ourselves a stringent and uncompromising strictness. Toward the love and piety that guides and counsels us, let our humble response be gentle and obedient in all. If either of these is lacking, I do not hope for a youth's perseverance in this way because of slothfulness and luke-warmness. Or I fear ruin because of rashness. The whole discernment of beginners ought to be to make themselves fools in all things for Christ and to depend on the judgment of another especially if they have such a senior who is known for certain to learn from God what he teaches. . . . Let them strive above all to drill themselves constantly in the obedience of which it is written: "Purify your hearts in the obedience to charity — for this is God's will, good, pleasing and perfect."

In order to obtain and keep these dispositions, the constant sentries of unremitting and persevering prayer must be sought. In this prayer faith is such that it hopes for all things, devotion such that it seems to constrain God, and love such that everything it seeks it feels it obtains in the prayer itself. And humility is such a thing of grace that in all things it prefers that God's will, not its own, be done. Let us strive at this stage to embrace purity of heart, cleanness of body, silence or well-ordered speech, eyes that are controlled and not looking around, and ears that are not itching. Let us be temperate in food and sleep, which helps rather than impedes a good day's work. Our hands should be under control and our gait appropriate. Rather than a lustful laughter, let us grace all with a gentle smile. Let us practice spiritual meditation assiduously and engage in well-chosen reading, not that born of curiosity. . . . A serene face should bespeak the kindness that is in our heart for everyone. Let us be generous in our work. This stage is the time and place for cutting off indulgent pleasures, for rooting out all vices and for crushing evil desires.

At this stage, those who love more push ahead more. At this stage there is labor, at this stage work!

Those who wish to make progress in great things must be faithful in small. In that area where through the largess of the Creator we already have the right of control, namely over our own bodies, let us manifest a good will and do what the apostle Paul says: "I speak in human terms on account of the weakness of your flesh. Just as you formerly yielded your members to serve impurity and iniquity upon iniquity, so now yield your members to serve uprightness for sanctification." It is as if he were saying: When love has passed into charity, when the soul has attained to perfect purity, then will I tell you or point out to you something exceedingly different and divine. For now, receive what is human. Formerly by your negligence and sins you were separated from what made you right with God, yielding your members to the service of sin in everything. To iniquity everything, to righteousness nothing. Now may you yield your members to serve what is right for sanctification. . . .

By all this, things begin to take on a new countenance for the young. The better charisms, which they have labored until now to emulate, of themselves begin to appeal to them in a more familiar way. The body, humbled by holy discipline, begins to pass from habits, however good, to the spontaneous service of the spirit. The inner countenance of these new persons begins to be renewed day by day until it is unveiled to behold the good things of God. . . . As a result these young ones, laboring for so long now, begin to gather some unwonted and sweet affections. They comfortably rest in them when they are present. When they are taken away and do not return at their wish, the youths feel tormented. When they first begin to taste these affections they are like peasants who were raised in the country and nourished on country cooking. That is what they were used to, and now for the first time they enter a royal banquet hall. When they are ignominiously chased away and thrown out with some violence, they can hardly bring themselves to return to the house of their poverty. They return time after time to the royal door, importuning, persistent and eager as one in need. As a beggar, hoping and sighing, they look up whenever the door is opened to see if anything is going to be offered to them. And sometimes by their shamelessness and importunity, they have so overcome and overstepped all hurdles in their desire, that they leap up to wisdom's inmost table and impudently take a seat like a guest, sure to be turned out. But they may hear: "Eat, friends, drink! Drink freely, my dearest friends!"

Temptation

At this point, unless those in this youthful stage are on their guard, the weighty hindrance of temptation befalls them. This either seriously slows down the way in which they have till now been happily moving ahead or it may turn them back to a sort of lethargy of lukewarmness. What they have received for the journey from their devoted Father to prevent them from succumbing on the way, they begin to consider adequate. They settle where they are. And it is there, where they fail to advance, that they really begin to fail. They abuse the grace of God. From it, but actually against it, they forge an empty self-confidence . . . . They put their trust in the execution of their own will and not in the Lord.

Charity, the Adult Stage

The person, full of good hope, whose youth God makes happy, begins to grow into a perfect adult, into the measure of the age of the fullness of Christ. For now love begins to be strengthened and illumined and to become a real driving force. It receives the name of a virtue that is more powerful and of greater dignity. Yes, this enlightened love is charity: a love from God, in God, for God. Yes, charity is God. Scripture tells us: "God is charity." A brief enough statement, but it tells all. Whatever can be said of God can be said of charity. According to its nature, the nature of the Giver, it is a substance; according to its nature as gift, it is a quality of the soul. Though for emphasis, God himself is called the gift of charity. The virtue of charity is above all the other virtues; it clings to God and is made like unto him.

What shall we say about charity? We have heard of it but we have not known it, we have not seen it. The apostle Paul knew it. He outdid himself in praising it, extolling it as the more excellent way:

> I show you a yet more excellent way. If I speak with the tongues of humans and angels and do not have charity, I become like sounding brass or a tinkling cymbal. And if I should have prophecy and should recognize all mysteries and all knowledge, and if I have faith so complete that I could move mountains and do not have charity, I am nothing. And if I should distribute all my goods to feed the poor, and if I should deliver my body to be burned and do not have charity, it profits me nothing. Charity is patient, it is kind. Charity does not envy, does not deal perversely, is not puffed up, is not ambitious. It does not seek its own, is not provoked to anger. It thinks no evil, does not rejoice in iniquity; it rejoices in truth. It suffers all things, believes all things, hopes all things, bears all things. Charity never fails even if prophecies be made void or tongues cease or knowledge be destroyed. Now there remain faith, hope and charity, these three. But the greatest of these is charity.

This is the Lord's sweet yoke and light burden. This burden bears the bearer and lightens the load. This light burden of the gospel is sweet to those to whom the Lord himself says: "I will call you no longer servants but my friends." Those who had not formerly been able to bear the precepts of the law now find the precepts of the gospel light by reason of cooperating grace. Those who could not at first fulfill, "You shall not kill," now find it easy to lay down their life for their sisters and brothers. And so on for the rest. A heavy burden is placed on a mule, and it refuses it as unbearable. Then a four-wheeled wagon is brought in (the gospel traversing all the world); the mule now transports twice the weight without effort. Again, a little bird cannot lift itself up without feathers and wings. But add the weight of feathers and wings and it soars without effort. So, too, hard dry bread cannot go down. But soak it in milk or another liquid and it is easily swallowed. . . .

The permanence of charity

Charity is one thing, a passing affective movement another. Charity possesses the soul as a kind of orientation and abiding virtue, firm, stable and maintained by grace. Feelings of affection change according to various occurrences and times. The weakness of the flesh, due especially to original sin, often offends, often fails, often seriously wounds. We are wounded when, more passive than active, we suffer interiorly and wrongly what is committed exteriorly by the flesh. We do not lose charity but sigh and call out to God through charity: "Unhappy person that I am, who shall deliver me from the body of this death?" For this reason the apostle Paul says: "I myself serve the law of God with my mind, but my flesh serves the law of sin." And again: "It is not I who do it but the sin that dwells in me." Therefore those who are, as John says, born of God, that is, according to the reckoning of the inner person, do not sin insofar as they hate rather than approve the sin which the body performs exteriorly. They are preserved inwardly by the seed of spiritual birth by which they are born of God. If they are occasionally wounded and weakened by the onslaught of sin, nevertheless they are not destroyed when the roots of their charity are very deeply fixed. They instead rise up and recover, becoming more fruitful and alive in the hope of good fruit. As John says: "All who are born of God do not sin, for God's seed abides in them and they cannot sin because they are born of God." The force of these words ought to be considered. He says: "They do not sin because anyone who is born of God endures rather than commits sin." And they cannot sin, that is, persevere in sin, while they are hastening to subject even their flesh to the law of God whom they serve in their minds, even though they may seem to serve the law of sin in enduring the onslaughts of sin and temptation.

Peter, when he sinned, did not lose charity. For he sinned more against truth than against charity when he lied by saying with his mouth that he did not belong to him to whom he belonged wholly in his heart. Therefore charity's truth immediately washed away with tears falsehood's denial.

David, too, when he sinned did not lose charity. Rather, the charity in him was somehow stunned by the vehement sting of temptation. Charity in him was never abolished but it was, as it were, somehow dazed. It woke up soon enough at the voice of the accusing prophet. He broke forth immediately in that confession of a very ardent charity: "I have sinned against the Lord." And he deserved to hear at once: "The Lord also has taken away your sin. You shall not die."

The relationship of faith, hope and charity

Continuing in the praise of charity: Love is in faith and in hope. Charity is in itself and of itself. It is possible that faith and hope exist without charity, but that charity not contain faith and hope within itself is not possible. Faith posits the existence of what is loved. Hope promises it. A person who loves, therefore, loves in faith and in hope. Only what is believed in and hoped for can be loved. But charity already in some way possesses, already holds, already embraces what is believed and hoped for. As a result love desires to see the God of faith and hope because it loves. Charity loves because it sees. It is the eye by which God is seen.

The soul possesses its own senses. . . . By the instrumentality of life, the body is joined to the soul through the five senses of the body. Through the instrumentality of charity, the soul is joined to God by the five spiritual senses.

The love of parents is compared to touch, for this impulse is spontaneous to all and is in some way ordinary and palpable. It is present and offers itself to everyone by a natural encounter that we cannot escape even if we want to. The sense of touch encompasses all one's physical being and is activated by contact with any other physical object. In order for there to be touch, one or both bodies must be alive. Just as, no matter where we turn, our body cannot be without touch, so our soul cannot be without this impulse. On account of this, this love is not highly recommended in the scriptures. Rather, it is to be restrained lest it become excessive. As the Lord says: "If anyone does not hate his father and mother he cannot be my disciple."

Secondly, social love, the love of brothers and sisters, the love of the holy catholic Church is compared to taste. Of this it is written: "Behold how good and how pleasant it is for brothers and sisters to dwell together in unity." Just as life is ministered to in the body through taste, so in this love the Lord has commanded blessings and life. Although taste is exercised physically, it nevertheless generates an inner savor which affects the soul. . . . Social love, because it is linked and nourished by mutual duties through physical cohabitation in unity, through like professions, through similar studies and many other such doings, seems to be more a thing of the instinct. Yet to a large degree it is spiritual. . . .

Thirdly, to the sense of smell is compared natural love,

which naturally loves every person without any expectation of recompense because of a likeness in nature and because of companionship. This love comes from the depths of our nature and impregnates our soul so that nothing human is foreign to us. . . .

Fourthly, spiritual love, love of our enemies, is compared to hearing. Hearing involves nothing interior, that is, it does not take place inside the body. It is instead, in a way, exterior, a vibration on the eardrum. It calls the soul to come out and listen. So, too, no natural impulse in the heart, no compelling need stimulates love of enemies. It is the fruit of obedience, which is signified by hearing. This love is said to be spiritual in that it promotes likeness to the Son of God and the dignity of the children of God. The Lord says: "Do good to those who hate you that you may be children of your Father in heaven," and so on.

Fifthly, divine love is compared to vision. As vision is the principal sense, so divine love holds primacy among all the affections. All the other senses are said to see through the vision of the eyes although only the eye sees. We say: Touch and see, taste and see, and so on. So, too, all things which are rightly loved are said to be loved by divine love, since it is clearer than light that nothing should be loved except for God's sake, and that each object is loved not so much for the sake of the thing itself that is loved but more on account of why it is loved. . . . Sight is indeed a power of the soul, untainted, strong and pure. So, too, divine love is powerful because it accomplishes great things. It is pure because, as someone has said, "Nothing defiled enters into it." For God does not deign to be loved along with some other thing which is not loved on account of him. Sight is located in the foremost part of the body, in the chief and conspicuous place of the head. Even according to the shape of this body, sight has beneath itself the organs of all the other senses according to their order, dignity and capacity for virtue. The closer these senses are to sight the more a thing of the soul they are; the further away, the more physical they are. Touch is the least spiritual of all the senses and more undistinguished than the rest; it is given to every part of the body though it properly belongs to the hands.

The mind, which is the summit of the soul, ought so to be the seat of God's love that it may have under it all the other loves and rule over them and illumine them. Nor may there be anything in them which hides from its heat and light. . . . So the illumined love of God acquires its own seat in Christians to move them toward some likeness to the divine power, all the while making every finite and limited creature seem as nothing in comparison to God. Love trusts that all that is the Father's is its own and that all things work together for its good, whether Paul or Cephas, life or death, things present or things to come. All things belong to love, and the riches of the whole world belong to the faithful.

Love and reason

The sight for seeing God, the natural light of the soul created by the Author of nature, is charity. There are, however, two eyes in this sight, always throbbing with a natural intensity to perceive the light that is God: love and reason. When one attempts to look without the other, it does not get very far. When they help one another, they can do much. Then they become the single eye of which the Bridegroom in the Canticle says: "You have wounded my heart, O my Friend, with one of your eyes." They labor much, each in its own way. One of them, reason, cannot see God except to perceive what he is not. Love cannot bring itself to rest except in what he is. What can reason apprehend or discover about which it can say: Is this my God?

Reason is only able to discover what God is to the extent
that it discovers what he is not. Reason has its own set paths
and ways by which it progresses. Love, however, advances
more by its shortcomings and apprehends more by its
ignorance. Reason, therefore, seems to advance through
what God is not toward what God is. Love, putting aside
what God is not, rejoices to lose itself in what he is. From
God love has come forth, and it naturally aspires to return
to its source. Reason has greater sobriety, love greater
happiness. Nevertheless, as I have said, when they help one
another, when reason teaches love and love enlightens
reason, and reason merges into the impulse of love and love
lets itself be confined within the limits of reason, then they
can do great things. But what is it they can do? Just as
anyone who progresses in this cannot make progress and
learn except through experience, so understanding of this
cannot be communicated to an inexperienced person. As it
is said in the Book of Wisdom: "In one's joy the stranger
shall not meddle."

Up till now we have been delicately nourished by sweetness and the delights of love and sometimes bruised by the
disciplines of paternal piety. Now we are invaded by a love
strong as death, and the sweet sword of love cuts us free
from love and attraction for the world just as death frees us
from the body. . . . By its death the body is deadened to all
its senses. The soul, by this death, advances the more and
is quickened and strengthened in all its senses, advancing
now firmly, steadily and prudently in its ways and in all its
steps. Until now, prevented on all sides by ignorance, doubt
and wavering, it scarcely dared to step forward and consent
to the good. . . .

The impulse of charity adheres indissolubly to God, and
all the mind's judgments are made according to the light of
his countenance so that it can do exteriorly what the good
and pleasing will of God indicates interiorly. We thus find

delight in always straining toward the face of God and in it to read and to understand, as in the Book of Life, the laws by which we must live to illumine faith, to strengthen hope and to enkindle charity.

The Spirit of knowledge openly teaches the pious what to do and how to do it. The Spirit of fortitude confers the strength and power to accomplish this. The Spirit of counsel gives the right dispositions. And when we are free to be free in God, to cleave to God, we are made like unto God through the piety of devotion and unity of will. But when we are compelled to return to human discourse and human affairs by the law of the face of God, we bring to others a face radiant with that oil of God's charity both in our actions and in our words and even in a sort of glorification, a grace that flows into our outer presence.

The Wisdom of Old Age

The wisdom of the person making progress takes up the rest of the journey. It does not reject charity or leave it behind but helps it along. Yet wisdom is tired of carrying charity's baggage. Having other things in view it attempts to prepare itself and get itself ready to enter into the joy of the Lord. It hates taking on any cares at all. When it does take on some labors, it does not like to be preoccupied with them. There is no lack of strength to carry them, but it flees from the impediment. To encourage the pious to progress at this stage and to incite them to enter into his joy, the Lord says: "You shall love the Lord your God with your whole soul, with your whole heart, with your whole strength and with all your mind."

Four movements toward God are demanded from us in

their entirety. In that he says "with your whole heart" he claims for himself the whole will; "with your whole soul," all our love. "With your whole strength" he speaks of charity; "with all your mind," the enjoyment of wisdom. First the will moves us toward God, then love carries us forward, charity contemplates and wisdom enjoys.

Wisdom is rightly placed in the mind. Since what is called the mind is that which remembers or that which is eminent in the soul, it is well to ascribe to it that power which is preeminent above all the soul's other powers. For the mind is the particular power of the soul whereby we cleave to God and enjoy God. This enjoyment is a sort of divine savor, so the word wisdom (*sapientia*) comes from savor (*sapor*). This savor is a sort of tasting. And none are worthy to speak of this tasting except those who have deserved to taste. As scripture says: "Taste and see that the Lord is sweet." By this tasting, according to the apostle Paul, one tastes the good word of God and the riches of the world to come.

But we must inquire more subtly into this taste which has that savor whereby wisdom savors. First, it must be said that although those who ascend will come to the peak of wisdom by degrees, nevertheless, at every degree even up to the last, wisdom, as she herself says in the book bearing her name, seeks out those seeking her and goes to meet them in the streets, joyfully showing herself to them. Otherwise, the will would not move or love make progress or charity advance to contemplation or wisdom to enjoyment. Therefore, as we have begun, let us pursue our investigation of taste.

The Body of Christ is the universal Church of the Old and New Testaments. In the head of this body, that is, the first and older and superior part which is the primitive Church, there are four senses: sight, hearing, smell and touch. The eyes are the angels because of the loftiness of contemplation. The ears are the patriarchs because of the virtue of obedience. The nose or smell is the prophets because of their awareness of absent realities. Touch is a sense common to all. All these senses were in the head before the advent of the Mediator, but they were languishing. The lower body was thoroughly dead because of the absence of one sense, taste. Without its support the body was not able to live nor the senses obtain the strength of their own aliveness.

Taste is located in the throat, on the boarder of the head and the body as if connecting both. It symbolizes him who by taking flesh was made a little less than the angels and Moses and Elijah and the other patriarchs and prophets. By showing patience and humility he has made himself somehow still less and more abased. . . .

Coming after the prophets and patriarchs as the boundary line between the law and grace, between the head and the body, he brought out, through the mystery of his humanity, his passion and resurrection, whatever in the law and the prophets and the psalms was vital and useful for the body. The man-Christ did this as if tasting in his mouth, that is, by understanding in and through himself and then conveying to the body the things to be understood. By a sort of interior savor of divinity, Christ, the wisdom of God, was made wisdom for us. He has things that are savory. He makes them savory and useful for us. He has life in himself, and through himself he invigorates and strengthens the entire body. He gives joy to himself and joy to the angels by bringing his body to perfect fullness. He gives joy to the patriarchs and to the prophets by the vision of his own day as he himself said: "Abraham your Father rejoiced that he might see my day. He saw it and was glad." Joy and life for the whole body! So, with minds dancing, as we are brought to life and strengthened by this spiritual taste, let us shout out what we have heard and seen and our hands have handled, something of the Word of life. This is why we submit all our prayers through Christ our Lord. Either we direct all our prayers and sacrifices to God our Father through him as through our mediator, or we hope for the best of gifts, for every perfect gift, from the Father of lights through him, our Mouth and our Taste and our Wisdom. . . .

This is the taste which the Spirit of understanding gives us in Christ: the understanding of scripture and of the sacraments of God. So it was when the Lord appeared to his disciples after the resurrection. As the evangelist says, "He opened to them the meaning that they might understand the scripture." For when we begin not only to understand but even somehow to touch and handle the inner meaning of scripture and the power of God's mysteries and sacraments with the hand of experience, then at last wisdom accomplishes what is proper to it. This does not happen except by some special consciousness, by the discipline of an experience of understanding which reads inwardly within the experience itself and senses the goodness and effective power within the sons and daughters of grace. Then wisdom judges those who are worthy, and by its anointing it teaches them all things. Then it imprints itself in us by affixing the seal of God's goodness in us. It conforms to itself by this anointing everything within us, making us peaceful and gentle. If it finds any hardness, any rigidity, it pounds and crushes it. Having received this health-giving happiness of God and having been strengthened by the spirit of wisdom, the holy soul joyfully sings to God: "The light of your countenance, O Lord, is upon us. You have given gladness to my heart." This is why the Lord says: "This is eternal life, that they may know you, the only true God, and Jesus Christ whom you have sent."

O blessed knowledge wherein is contained eternal life! That life comes from this tasting, because to taste is to understand. The least of the apostles, filled, exhilarated and strengthened in this wisdom through the savor of this tasting, says: "To me, the least of all the saints, is given this grace: to preach among the Gentiles the unsearchable riches of Christ and to enlighten all, that they may see the sacrament which has been hidden from eternity in God who created all things. Thus the manifold wisdom of God is made known to the principalities and powers in heavenly places and throughout the Church according to the eternal purpose which was in Christ Jesus our Lord. In him we have boldness. Through faith in him we have confident access to God." Paul says a little further on: "For this cause I bend my knees to the Father of our Lord Jesus Christ after whom all paternity in heaven and on earth is named, that he would grant you according to the riches of his glory to be strengthened by his Spirit with might within, that Christ may dwell by faith in your hearts. Thus being rooted and founded in charity you may be able to comprehend with all the saints what is the breadth and length and height and depth." Let us freely consider this to see if perhaps we are able to penetrate to some extent the meaning of this apostolic wisdom!

Christ our mediator

To God's four attributes: power, wisdom, charity and truth (or eternity, which is the same, for nothing is true unless it be unchanging) we are doubly obligated to respond. To the power which can punish us and to the wisdom from which nothing can hide, we owe true fear, that is, a fear which the laziness of false security or the refuge of pretense does not undermine. Pretense is present when we feign the effort to keep the commandments or when we attribute to God an irrational mercy. To charity and to truth we owe true love, that is, a love which is not undermined by the lukewarmness of affections or a nagging mistrust. For what is owed charity except charity? Indeed, the truth of charity and the charity of truth removes every scruple of mistrust, mistrust that charity be not loving, truth be deceiving or eternity fail. For this reason Paul says: "That you may be able to comprehend with all the saints what is the breadth and length and height and depth." In height note power, in depth wisdom, in breadth charity and in length eternity or truth. This is the cross of Christ! . . .

The Trinity took counsel together, that counsel about which the prophet says: "May your ancient counsel be made true." The Lord indeed saw how confused everything was, how disturbed for us. Nothing held its own place, nothing its own order. He saw that we had strayed so far into the region of unlikeness that by ourselves we were not able nor did we know how to return. The angel had presumed to likeness to God, saying: "I will place my seat in the north, I will be like the Most High." Similarly Adam desired to be like God. He was persuaded: "You shall be as gods." Does God the Father therefore say: My Son, the splendor of my glory and the figure of my substance will have many rivals, equals and companions? Both the angel and Adam have been cast down. God the Son, the image of God, saw that both the angel and Adam were made like unto him, that is, to the image of God, but not as he, the image of God. He saw that they had perished through an inordinate appetite for his image and likeness. And he said: Misery alone is never envied. Men and women should be assisted as justice does not prohibit assisting them. Therefore, I shall show myself to them as a man despised and the least of all, a man of sorrows and knowing infirmity, that they may be zealous to imitate my humility through which they will come to the glory toward which they are striving. They will hear from me: "Learn of me because I am meek and humble of heart and you shall find rest for your souls."

The manner of redemption

So the Son of God girded himself in this way and drew near through humility to save those who were to be saved, those who had perished through pride. Making himself the mediator between God and the human family . . . he was made human. "And there came forth a rod out of the root of Jesse and a flower shall rise up out of his root. And the spirit of the Lord shall rest upon him, the spirit of wisdom and of understanding, the spirit of counsel and of fortitude, the spirit of knowledge and of piety. And he shall be filled with the spirit of the fear of the Lord. . . ." Our most powerful athlete, having entered as it were the stadium of the world, was anointed with the oil of the Holy Spirit for the match. He rejoiced as a giant to run the course laid out for humans. Mark how the prophet began with the higher gifts and moved toward the lower when announcing the descent of the Mediator. We, on the contrary, seeking through the same graces of the Holy Spirit and the work of this Mediator a return to the higher ones, begin from the lowest, that is, from fear.

Christ had fear for the Father but a chaste, filial fear through which he offered the Father honor in all things, saying: "My food is to do the will of my Father who is in heaven," or as in the psalm: "Let my heart rejoice that I may fear your name," and many other things like this. He was seen to abase himself through this fear, to humble himself, to disregard himself that he might restore to the Father, reclaimed and renewed, the work which the Father had done through him but which had perished.

In this way our Mediator had fear toward the Father as if toward one above him and piety toward the miserable creature to be reconciled as one beneath him. Of both he had knowledge, knowing what is to be shown to each. To carry out the ministry of his mediation, although he had from above the good will of his Father, he had nothing from the wretch groveling here below. Since reason and the way of mediation require that something be had, from the one below he demanded faith. He demanded faith by first reaching out to us with his grace. Nothing could be more reasonable than his demand, for it was not difficult for us miserable ones to trust in him by whom we see ourselves first embraced by his graciousness. But since none can believe in him without hope, for who would believe in someone in whom they did not hope, with faith he brought hope. And with hope he added fear. Without fear there could be no real hope that one would never be deserted by so gracious a Mediator.

The Mediator, having received from the accused this pledge for salvation, returns to his Father. He goes up into the mountain alone to pray. In agony he prays the longer, sweating blood. "Father," he prays, "glorify your Son." Here is what I offer you. Here is what I shall offer them. Here is what I have from you. Here is what I have from them. I am the mediator and the reasons for my mediation already seem to speak for their salvation. . . . For I know what I am doing. Innocent, I will die for the guilty. My goodness can do incomparably more than the malice of the enemy, the punishment of my innocence more than the punishment of human disobedience. The Father says: "I have glorified and I will glorify him."

Now the most powerful Mediator needs the spirit of counsel, because if the prince of this world had understood, he would never have crucified the Lord of Glory. Therefore, he hid the power of his divinity from the evil one throughout and let him see only the weakness of innocent flesh. . . . The old deceiver, having been deceived, inflicted on the Mediator, to whom it was in no way due, the punishment for sin, a very cruel death. . . .

Taking his own body and blood in his hands, the Media-

tor said: "Eat this. Drink this. And live by it." And present-
ing these to his Father, he says: "Behold, Father, the price
of my blood. If you require a price for sin, see here is my
blood for it. . . ."

We have been satiated with the fruit of this work by the
Mediator, the wisdom of God. Not only are we reconciled
but we are wise as well, for we savor what we eat. We eat
and drink the Redeemer's body and blood, the heavenly
manna, the bread of angels, the bread of wisdom. And while
eating it we are transformed into the nature of the food we
eat. For to eat the body of Christ is nothing other than to
be made the body of Christ and the temple of the Holy
Spirit. . . .

This is the wisdom about which the apostle Paul says:
"We speak wisdom among the perfect." Of it we speak as
those who have heard and have not seen, as we would speak
about some city we had not seen but about which we have
heard many things. Yet one who had seen it would speak
about it very differently and more descriptively. . . . Wisdom always overcomes cunning. Dwelling together with
God, wisdom knows how always to advance and never to
slacken. It reaches from end to end mightily and orders all
things gently. It wisely gives itself to divine things, cau-
tiously to physics, prudently to morals.

Consequently, the wise once cleansed from all extraneous
attachments and savoring only God, lay bare what is within.
Oriented completely to God in all things, they attend to
every creature under God but not in a manner other than
God attends to them: disposing and ordering all things in
the light and virtue of wisdom. They act in the same way,
judge in the same way as they are and as they live. They
form true judgments and are right with God from whom
they are and live. For wisdom is, she says it herself, "the
radiance of the eternal light and the unspotted mirror of
God's majesty." She is the genuine emanation of the bright-

ness of almighty God and the breathing out of his virtue. Therefore the wise bear within themselves the radiance of eternal light and the mirror of God's majesty. When wisdom exposes herself to a creature, she expresses and shows forth the image of the goodness and righteousness of God. And just as the creature is breathed upon inwardly by the power of God, so it pours forth outwardly the emanation of the brightness and charity of God. . . .

Therefore, those enlightened by the spirit of wisdom, love justice and hate iniquity. Because of this God has anointed them with the oil of gladness with which Christ had been anointed before them, those sharing in him whom God has soaked with grace. They please all and are loved by all. Even those who are against them, seeing these effects, fear and revere them. . . . Having received this grace whereby they dwell in unity among themselves in God and enjoy God in themselves, they sense that all the contradictions of the flesh have disappeared. The result is that the flesh is not in them except as an instrument of good work. For although they waste away gradually because of the flesh's miseries and infirmities, by this very fact they grow stronger in the inner person. "For when I am weak then I am strong," says the apostle Paul. They perceive near themselves some new spiritual grace. Their eyes are simple, their ears tempered. Sometimes in the fervor of prayer there is a wisp of fragrance of an unfamiliar scent. There is such a taste of sweetness that it cannot be tasted. There is through mutual touch such an incentive to charity that they seem to themselves to bring forth from within themselves a paradise of spiritual delight. Their countenance along with the bearing of their whole body, with the seemliness of their life, manners and activities in their mutual service, devotion, and gracious acceptance of one another unite and bind them one to another in this particular gracefulness. Thus they truly are one heart and one soul. Surely by such purity of conscience and the

grace of a communal way of life they are already beginning
here that future glorification of their bodies which they will
enjoy perfectly in the unending life to come. . . . In that life,
God will be seen by each person to be in all and be seen by
all in each person. Not that divinity may be seen by physical
eyes, but the glorified body by some grace manifested
through it will make known the presence of divinity. In this
life religion with its physical sacraments is effective for this.
Since we understand scarcely anything besides bodies and
physical things while we are passing through, we are bound
by the physical sacraments lest we draw away from God.
(Hence religion is said to derive from *religare*, to bind.)
However, once the faithful have been taught by such things,
they should begin not to need them and to pass from the
physical to the spiritual and from the spiritual to the Maker
of the spiritual and physical. Truly, then, they shall leave
their baggage behind. For having left the body and all bodily
cares and hindrances, they forget everything except God
and attend to nothing except God alone. As if regarding
themselves and God alone, they say: "My beloved is mine
and I am his. For what have I in heaven? And besides you
what have I wanted upon earth? For you my flesh and my
heart fainted away. You are the God of my heart, the God
that is my portion forever."

The consummation

Then we come to death. This transitus to life wretched
infidels call death. Yet what do the faithful call it if not a
passover? In bodily death we die perfectly to the world that
we may live perfectly in God. We enter the wondrous
tabernacle. We enter all the way to the house of God. As
we said at the beginning, when all things go well and
according to order, a natural force bears each to its proper

place. The body returns to the earth from which it was taken
and the spirit returns to God who created it.

But what is this transitus to God? Once all obligations
have been severed and all hindrances overcome, in perfect
happiness and unfailing love the saints cling completely to
God. Even more, they are so truly united to God that they
become those of whom it is said: "I have said: You are gods
and children of the Most High." This is the destination of
those who set Jerusalem before their eyes as the beginning
of their gladness, those whom the unction of the Holy Spirit
teaches all things. They wisely arrange ascents in their
hearts from virtue to virtue until they see the God of gods
in Sion, the God of gods, the beatitude of the blessed, the
joy of those who rejoice as they ought, the one good, the
highest good of all. From the goal of good intention at the
beginning of the ascent until this goal of complete consummation is reached, wisdom strongly extends support, pro-
tecting the fortitude of the climbers lest they fall during the
ascent. Wisdom gently disposes all things, both the adver-
sities and the things that go well, modifying and organizing
all things for them toward the good until they are led back
to their beginning and are hidden in the hiddenness of the
face of God.

Every wise climber must know, however, that the stages
of this ascent are not like the rungs of a ladder in the sense
that each single step of love is necessary in its own time and
not at other times. Every single degree of love does indeed
have its own time and place in the order of ascent whereby
it is seen more clearly to pursue its own purposes with the
cooperation of all the other degrees. But they all nonetheless concur and work together. Sometimes one particular
degree leads. Sometimes it follows. Often the first becomes
the last and the last first.

Help for the Beginner on the Way

In the first days of the holy leisure William found when he was finally freed from the burdens of the abbatial office and settled in the solitude of Signy, he gathered up the jottings he had made through the years. His abiding concern for the young impelled him to assemble his notes in a collection of "meditations" aimed at helping beginners in their first steps along the way of prayer.

One of the things that strikes us as we read these is how abundantly William uses images drawn from nature, what is experienced in daily life—a good place to meet the beginner. So in Meditation Two we find him speaking of dogs and their relation to their masters, the darkness of night and the dawn, the rising sun, the whole experience of waking up, the falcon so common in medieval hunting, the spring in the valley and the dryness of the desert.

In the course of the meditations William traces out the spiritual journey. It begins, of course, with God and his grace — and that is where it will end. Grace begets in us the humility to be open to authority from which faith receives the teaching to direct reason, which goes on to seek understanding. But understanding of the things of God can only come from God through the gifts. The dark nights of sense and spirit popularized later in the beautiful poetry of John of the Cross are graphically depicted in William's second meditation.

Though William constantly urges us on to more spiritual or transcendent prayer, nonetheless he does not rule out meditation on the sacred humanity of our Lord Jesus. Indeed the touching passages on the Lord and especially on his passion in Meditation Eight make it very evident that William himself spent a good bit of time allowing the experiences of Jesus' life to speak to him and call him forth.

Yet, even for the beginner William dares to trace out the full meaning of transforming union, *unitas spiritus*, union of spirit with God, "for to see God . . . is faith's proper desire." It is by love, the sense of the soul, that we are transformed into what we love, not in nature but in affection. But in this life God can only be perceived "as in a riddle." So we depend on the understanding that comes from above, the action of the gifts of the Holy Spirit. "This understanding serves to soothe the loving spirit, for there is clearly nothing in it of that which God is not and, although it is not wholly what God is, it is not different from that Reality." As we thus taste and see how gracious the Lord is "all of a sudden our whole being grows so sweet in tasting of his sweetness, and we are so lit up by seeing the light of his truth, we are beside ourselves in the joy of the Holy Spirit at this sudden plenitude of the highest good."

William knew these very high points. But he also knew that they passed quickly enough in this life leaving us only a memory and a confidence that we "will have won eternal life if this experience be perfected." And he knew the low points and the struggles of life, the struggle to know and to do the will of God. The very graphic struggle toward discernment found in Meditation Eleven, where it is described as an inner dialogue among one's intents, joints, marrow, soul and spirit, not only gives us a vivid picture of what William went through when deciding to embrace a more contemplative life as a Cistercian. It can also be helpful and encouraging for one engaged in a similar struggle. The principles offered by "marrow" are useful and universally applicable.

Meditation Two
The Search for God

Our search for God is urged on by the Scriptures and divine touches
in spite of our lethargy and sensuality.

"Come unto him and be enlightened, and your face shall
not be ashamed." But I am ashamed, O Lord, and confounded with a hideous and terrible confusion as often as I
come to you and find the door of vision shut. Almost I seem
to hear the fearful words: "Truly I tell you, I do not know
you." I desired that you would enlighten me, and now my
grief of heart and sore perplexity have thrown me into
darkness so complete that it almost seems it had been better
for me if I had not come.

For where shall I seek comfort, if desolation is your will
for me? Away with every consolation that neither is yourself
nor comes from you! May they perish! "Woe to the one
who is alone," says Solomon. Woe indeed to me if I be
alone, if you are not with me, nor yet I with you! I reckon
myself blessed, Lord, and highly blessed if I feel you with
me. But I am wearisome and hateful to myself whenever I
perceive that I am not with you. As long as I am with you
I am also with myself. I am no longer myself when I am not
with you. Woe is me whenever I am not with you, for no
existence is possible for me apart from you. I could not exist
in any way at all, either in body or in soul, save by your
constant power. I could not desire you, not seek you, save
by your ever present grace. And I could never find you, did
not your mercy and your goodness run to meet me on the
way. In all these things I am with you and I am conscious

of your grace at work in me. The fact that I exist and am alive seems good to me. My soul makes her boast in the Lord. But if, when you are present in thus doing good to me, I am myself absent from you in mind and heart, the operations of your grace it seems to me are like burial rites duly and carefully fulfilled upon a corpse.

Sometimes I feel you passing by. You do not stop for me but go straight on, leaving me crying after you like the Canaanite woman. And then, weary of the crying with which my misery importunes you, speaking as to a dog you reproach my sullied conscience with its past impurity and present shame. And you drive your dog from your table unfed and famished and beaten by the rebukes of its conscience. Or you just let it go. Should I draw near again when this occurs? Yes, surely, Lord. For the whelps that are chased with blows from their master's house return immediately. Hanging watchfully about the place, they receive their daily bread. I come again when I am driven out. Shut out, I howl. Beaten, I implore. A dog cannot live without a human's companionship nor can my soul without the Lord her God.

Open to me, therefore, Lord, that I may come to you and be enlightened by you. You dwell in your heavens, but you have made darkness your secret place, even the dark waters amid the clouds of the air. As the prophet says: "You have set a cloud before you so that our prayer may not pass through." But as for me, I have rotted on earth. I have made the thick and earthly covering of my heart more heavy even than it was before. Your heavenly stars do not shine for me. The sun is darkened and the moon gives no light. In psalms and hymns and spiritual songs I hear your mighty acts proclaimed. Out of your gospels your words and deeds shine forth for me, and the example of your servants strike unceasingly upon my eyes and ears. Your promises in scripture, the promises your truth has made, obtruding themselves without cease upon my sight and battering my deafness with their din, shake me with fear and taunt me. But long persistence in bad ways, along with very great insensibility of mind, has hardened me. I have learned to sleep with the sunshine full on my face and have grown used to it. I have become accustomed to not seeing what takes place before my eyes and, dead at heart as I am, though I am set in the midst of the sea, I have ceased to hear the roaring of its waves and the thunder of the sky.

How long, O Lord, how long? How long will you defer to rend the heavens and come down? How long will you delay to fulfill your wrath upon me and so to shatter my dullness that I may be no longer what I am but may know that it is you who rules Jacob and the utmost bounds of earth? Thus I will be turned, at least at eventide, and hunger like a dog that runs about your city—your city of which a portion sojourns still on earth but the greater part rejoices already in heaven. Maybe then I may find some who will receive my fainting soul into their habitation, my soul that has no couch of her own on which to lay her head.

Sometimes indeed I hear your Spirit's voice. Though no more than the whistling of a gentle air that passes me, I understand the message: "Come unto me and be enlightened." I hear and I am shaken. Arising as from sleep and shaking off my lethargy, a certain wonder fills me. I open my mouth and I draw in my breath? I stretch my spiritual muscles and rouse them from their sloth. I turn my back on the shades of night in which my conscience lies and come forth to the Sun of Righteousness who is rising now for me. But I am drowsy still, and the eyes of my reason are dazzled when I try to look at him. For they are used to darkness and unaccustomed to the light. And while both pupils and eyelids tremble and blink at the unwonted brightness, as best I can I wipe the rheum of my long sleep from them with the hand of exercise. If by your gift I find a fount of tears such as is wont to spring up speedily in lowly ground and in the valleys of a contrite soul, I wash the hands with which I work and the face I lift in prayer. Then, as the falcon spreads its wings toward the south to make its feathers grow, I stretch out my two hands to you, O Lord. My soul is as waterless ground in your sight and as desert land, unwatered and untrodden I appear before you in your holy place, that I may see your power and your glory. And when I raise to you the eyes of my mind and the perception of my reason, O Sun of Righteousness, it happens to me as is wont to happen to persons drunk with sleep or of weak eyes. Seeing one thing, they think that they are seeing two or three, until in the process of seeing it dawns upon them that the defect is in their sight and not in the thing seen. My soul has been used to find her pleasure through the senses and in things that they can apprehend. When it is roused from these preoccupations, I am immediately confronted with a mental picture that disturbs me with images derived from the senses. My powers of perception have been blunted by my former exclusive attention to sensible things with the result that now I do not know how to apprehend or think of anything except under such forms.

When I awake from the sleep of negligence I immediately direct my gaze on God. Concerning him the divine law instructs me: "Hear, O Israel! The Lord your God is one God." I fix my soul's regard entirely on him. I look to him for light, for I am about to worship or implore him. But I am confronted with the fact that God is Trinity. This mystery has been made known to me by the Catholic faith of my forebears. It has been impressed upon me by long use. It is commended to me by you yourself and those who teach your truth. But my soul's foolish way of picturing things sees and regards the Trinity in such a fashion that I contentedly entertain the concept that there is number in the simple being of the Godhead. In fact, it is beyond number although all it made has number and measure and weight. I think of the several Persons of the Trinity as having each his place and pray to the Father through the Son and in the Holy Spirit as though I pass from one to the other through the third. And so my mind, befogged by the one is scattered between the three, just as if there were three bodies to be differentiated or to be made one.

When the imagination or the mind thus envisages the Trinity, it does so in spite of itself. It suffers that mode of thought unwillingly and under protest; faith comes in and censures it. Reason through faith gives judgment. Authority condemns such imaginings. And all that is within me cries out what was said before: "Hear, O Israel! The Lord your God is one God!" For, although faith, reason and authority alike all teach me to think of the Father, the Son and the Spirit each by himself, they will allow in my thought of the Trinity no element whatever which either suggests division of the triune God's substance in time or place or number or seems to imply a confusion of the Persons. They so assert the unity of the Trinity as to rule out solitude. And the threefoldness of the Unity they so declare as to exclude from the being of God plurality of number. Your grace, O Lord, which precedes everything of worth in us, every capacity of skill or virtue, gives us some little knowledge of ourselves and you. And grace submits us to humility, humility to authority, authority to faith; faith teaches reason; reason, by means of faith, either refines the picture that the mind has formed or else destroys it and supplies another. Reason, however, does not teach faith in order to bring it to understanding. Rather through faith it looks for understanding to come down from above, from you, the Father of lights, from whom is every good and perfect gift. And the understanding which is not derived from reason nor reached by a process of thought but comes from the throne of your greatness as the reward of faith and is determined by your wisdom—that understanding is altogether like the fountain whence it springs. For, entering the mind of the believer, it takes reason to itself and makes it like itself. By it faith also is imbued with life and light.

Those about to pray to you, their God, stand there frightened and bewildered, holding themselves in their hands all the time that they may make themselves an offering to you. Fearful of that to which they have been used and dazed by things unwonted, they bear the signet of your faith with which to find you. But so far they have not found the way. They seek your face, O Lord, they seek your face, not knowing, yet not wholly ignorant of what they seek. The imaginings of their hearts concerning you they hate as idols. They love you as their faith presents you to them, but their minds fail to win the sight of you. Aflame with longing for your face, before which they would offer their sacrifice of righteousness and duty, their oblations and burnt offerings, they are more troubled when they are put off. And when for all their asking they still fail to win the light of faith from you in whom they trusted, they sometimes grow so disconcerted that they can hardly believe they believe in you at all. And they hate themselves, because it seems to them they have no love for you! But far be it from them, who are so anguished by desire for you that they should not believe in you or that they should not love you. They desire you to the exclusion of all things that are and even to the exclusion of themselves!

How long, O Lord, how long? If you do not light my candle, if you do not illuminate my darkness, I shall not be delivered from these straits, nor, save by you, my God, shall I surmount the wall.

Meditation Three
Seeking the Face of God

As painful as the incessant seeking be, the fullness it promises makes it altogether desirable so we are willing to leave behind all else.

I dare not now, Lord, look upon your face for all that I desire it even unto death. For you said to Moses: "No human shall see me and live." I do indeed desire to die that I may see or see that I may die. And yet I hide my face, as Moses did, not venturing to meet you eye to eye. For so it is written: "And Moses hid his face, for he dared not look upon the Lord." He would have looked upon the Lord, perhaps, if he had tried to see not who God is but what. For who God is he had already heard: "I am the God of Abraham, the God of Isaac and the God of Jacob."

And yet to this same Moses who, on hearing that his death was near, was all aflame with this selfsame desire and prayed that you would let him see your glory, you replied: "I will show you All Good." Where, Lord, is All Good, save in your face? That is why David, burning with the same desire, says: "You shall fill me with joy from your face."

Forgive me, Lord, forgive my heart's impatience for you. I seek your face, by your own gift I seek your countenance, lest you should turn it from me at the last.

I know indeed and I am sure that those who walk in the light of your countenance do not fall but walk in safety, and by your face their every judgment is directed. They are the living people, for their life is lived according to that which they read and see in your face as in an exemplar. O Lord, I dare not look upon your face against your will lest I be further confounded. Needy and beggared and blind, I stand in your presence, seen by you though I do not see you. And, standing thus, I offer you my heart full of desire for you, the whole of whatever I am, the whole of whatever I can do, the whole of whatever I know. I offer you the very fact that I so yearn and faint for you. But the way to find you, that I do not find.

Where are you, Lord, where are you? And where, Lord, are you not? This much at least I know, and that most certainly, that you in whom we move and have our being are in a manner present here with me and that from that most health-giving presence comes the longing and fainting of my soul for your salvation. I know in very truth, I am aware most healthfully, that you are with me. I know, I feel, I worship and I render thanks. But if you are with me, why am I not with you? What hinders it? What is the obstacle? What gets in the way? If you are with me, working for my good, why am I not in the same way with you, enjoying you, the supreme good of all? Is it because of my sins? But where is he who took them out of the way and nailed them to his cross? And surely it is not because I do not love him! Would I not die a hundred and a thousand times for you, Lord Jesus? If this is not enough for you, no more is it for me. Nothing satisfies my soul, nor do I seem to myself to love you at all, if I have not the joy of you. But I cannot so enjoy you until you grant me to see and know you after my own manner. But why do I not see you? As I now love you even unto death so would I love unto eternal life. Already, Lord, some of your nameless fragrance reaches me. If I could only sense it perfectly, I should search no more. You do indeed send me at times, as it were, mouthfuls of your consolation. But what is that for hunger such as mine? O you, Salvation of my soul, tell me, please tell me, why you have breathed this longing into me. Surely it is not merely to torment and rend and slay! And yet, if only it would slay! Lord, I implore you: Is this then my hell? Very well, so be it! Go on putting me to torture ceaselessly, and in that hell let me burn ceaselessly, knowing no respite from its pains one single day or hour or moment, even till I appear before your presence and behold your glory, and the eternal feast day of your face has shone upon my soul!

When Moses, Lord, of old covered his countenance and veiled his face before you, he symbolized the people under his command, who were forever fleeing from the face of God. But Paul, your Paul, who is all ours because he is all yours, the clarion voice of the New Testament, says of himself and those who follow him in their desire and love for you: "We all with unveiled face beholding the glory of the Lord are changed into the same image from glory to glory." That man of yours was fleeing to your face and not away from it.

Forgive, O Lord, forgive my boldness and my importunity. We dare so much only because we are consumed with longing. Your fire, that fire which you came to spread on earth and which you longed so greatly to see enkindled, that fire drives us. By your almightiest goodness, Lord, I pray you, by your most tender patience toward us, yield something to my quest and tell me what I desire when I seek your face. For so purblind am I, so vexed within myself that I am growing feeble even in my longing and do not know just what it is I long for. Do I desire to see you as you are? And what does "as" mean there? Does it mean "of what sort"? Or "how great"? But you, O Lord, are not of any "sort" nor have you measure. There is no quality nor quantity in you who are what you are. So "as you are," what does it mean? It is beyond our powers so to see you, for to see what you are is to be what you are. No one sees the Father but the Son, neither does any one see the Son except the Father. For this is to be the Father: to see the Son. And this is to be the Son: to see the Father. But the Lord adds: ". . . and the one to whom the Son shall have willed to reveal him." Now the Father and the Son have not two wills but one: the Holy Spirit. Through the Holy Spirit, therefore, the Triune God reveals himself to any friend of God on whom he would bestow special honor. But does anyone ever see God as the Father sees the Son or the Son the Father, who see each other, as we said, in such wise as to be not separate but one God? Yes, assuredly, but not in every way the same. . . .

To return to the sense of the soul, is it not of this that Paul is speaking when he says: "Beholding the glory of the Lord, we are changed into the same image"? That is how the soul's sense functions. For the soul's sense is love. By love it perceives whatever it perceives, alike when it is pleased and when it is offended. When the soul reaches out in love to anything, a certain change takes place in it by which it is made into the object loved. It does not become the same nature as that object, but by its affection it is conformed to what it loves. We cannot love a good person because that person is good, without being ourselves made good by that same goodness. Is not this the meaning of: "Think of the Lord in goodness," and "For to know you (i.e., Wisdom) is perception perfected." And also the words of the apostle Paul: "Let this mind be in you which was in Christ Jesus"? This is the charity by which one who loves "abides in God and God in that one."

O Charity, Charity, you have brought us to this that, because we love God and the Son of God, we are called and we are gods and the sons of God! Although "it does not yet appear what we shall be, when he shall appear we shall be like him for we shall see him as he is." Lord, it is good for us to be here! We wish we could stay here, we wish that we might die!

I beseech you, Lord, to grant to those who think and speak and write of you a balanced judgment, an utterance concise and disciplined and a heart aflame to find you, Jesus, in the scriptures that speak concerning you.

Forgive, O Lord, forgive. The love of your love drives me.

You know, you see how things are with me. I am no scrutinizer of your majesty. A pauper is what I am, seeking your grace. I beg you by the sweetness of your sweetest tenderness, do not let me be crushed by your majesty. Rather let me be supported by your grace. Forgive me, I say, for to see God—here in a riddle only but hereafter face to face—is faith's proper desire.

Do not flatter yourself, O human, do not be over-confident. Do not imagine you can stay here, however much you may be a person of desire like Daniel. Do not ever say: "It is enough!" Whatever awareness you have here of seeing God, whatever faith here teaches you about him, is a riddle, darker at times indeed, at others clearer. They only know who have experienced it, how sweet that vision is when it is present and how much it is to be desired when it seems to be withdrawn. For this experience is the stone with the name written upon it, which no one knows save the one who has received it.

And it is said of the vision that shall be face to face: "No one shall see me and live." For the one who sees will not live but will say: "O wretched one that I am! Who will deliver me from the body of this death?" hoping exceedingly that when at last one sees God perfectly then one will live indeed.

How does perception come into all this? Of what avail are mental images? Can reason or rational understanding effect anything? No. For although reason sends us to you, O God, it cannot of itself attain to you. Neither does that understanding which, as a product of reason, has lower matters for its place of exercise, go any further than does reason itself. It is powerless to attain to you. But the understanding which is from above carries the fragrance of its place of origin. There is nothing human in its operation, it is all divine. And where it is empowered it carries along with itself its own reasons, which function independently of the inferior reason except insofar as the obedience of faith requires.

This sort of understanding makes neither division nor conjunction in the Trinity. But when and how and as far as the Holy Spirit wills, it controls the believing mind so that something of what you are may be seen by those who in their prayer and contemplation have got past all that you are not, although they do not see you as you are. Nevertheless this understanding serves to soothe the loving spirit, for there is clearly nothing in it of that which you are not and, although it is not wholly what you are, it is not different from that Reality.

For the Spirit of the Lord of a sudden clothes the humble, tranquil person on whom he rests and so changes that one that no antithesis is felt in the believer's mind. The Trinity in no way contradicts the Unity nor does it put a stumbling block before the piety of the one who seeks the one God. The unity of substance does not dim the charity of the one who rejoices in the love between the Father and the Son. Neither the onlyness nor the plurality disturbs, but the oneness of the Trinity and the threefoldness of the Unity so avail that with a sober understanding, one comprehends the majesty of the divine incomprehensibility by the very fact that one does not comprehend it. And as one thus tastes and sees how gracious the Lord is, all of a sudden one's whole being grows so sweet in tasting of his sweetness and one is so lit up by seeing the light of his truth and so beside one's self in the joy of the Holy Spirit at this sudden plenitude of the highest Good, that one is confident that eternal life is won if this experience be perfected. For "this is life eternal, that they may know you the only true God and Jesus Christ whom you have sent." "Come to him," therefore, "and be enlightened and your faces shall not be ashamed."

Meditation Seven
The Face of God

In humility and love our face seeks the face of God, knowledge of his truth, which makes us know what we do not know.

"My heart has talked to you, my face has sought you. Your face, Lord, will I seek. Do not turn away your face from me. Do not shun your servant in wrath."

It seems surpassing boldness and effrontery to make comparison between my face and yours, Lord God! For you see and judge the hearts of all, and if you enter into judgment with your servant the face of my iniquity can only flee before that of your righteousness.

But if, in order to excuse and help my poverty, you should grant me burning love and dutiful humility, then let them flee who hate. I for my part should not flee your face. For love is very daring and humility fosters confidence. I am not conscious of these virtues in myself. Yet I avow myself your friend. For if you ask me: "Do you love me?" as you asked Peter, I shall say plainly, I shall tell you boldly: "Lord, you know all things, you know I want to love you." And that is as much as to say: "If you ask me the same thing a thousand times, I shall as often make the same reply: You know I want to love you." And that means that my heart desires nothing so much as it desires to love you. I cultivate humility as well, which those who make such definitions call contempt of one's own excellence. But as long as I continue sometimes to accede unthinkingly to certain small suggestions of my own superiority and fail to shake myself free of them with sufficient speed when they are offered me, then I know quite well I am not really humble.

There is another sort of humility—namely the knowledge of oneself. In that, if I am judged according to what I know

about myself, it is as they say all up with me. My appearance
before your just tribunal is ill-starred. But if the fact that
my sin is ever before me is judged a virtue in your sight, of
that I think I am not wholly destitute. For my inward gaze
turns so often to the foulness of my sins (even when I do
not want to think of them and am intent on better things)
that I detest myself because of it. O Lord, what more shall
I say about my shame-faced conscience? Whatever it is like,
whatever its condition, its whole face so desires yours that
it scorns and despises all the things of this life and even life
itself for the love of your face. It does not care a fig what
else it sees as long as it sees you.

Thus, O desire of my eyes, my face seeks you. I seek your
face. I implore you do not turn it from me. Teach me, O
eternal Wisdom, by the illumination of your countenance
what is that face of yours and what is mine. For though I
burn with desire to see you face to face, I do not know
enough yet of either yours or mine. I know well enough that
if it was not granted to the apostle Paul in this life to see
you face to face, and if your Beloved Disciple, loving and
loved as he was, was not allowed to see you as you are, then
a man who hopes and seeks to see you in that way is simply
not right in his head.

And yet, when I hear David speak of face to face, hearing
another hope in you, I cannot give up hope. And this is not
because I have forgotten who I am but because my trust is
in your tender mercy. Although I make poor progress in my
loving I would not like to love you less than any other lover
of yours does. For though it seems that Moses was denied
what David by no means despaired of attaining, David
himself sings and chants concerning this same Moses and
the other fathers that "they did not get possession of the
land through their own sword, neither was it their own arm
that saved them but your right hand and the light of your
face." And of himself he says: "O Lord, in your favor you

gave strength to my beauty. You turned your face from me and I was troubled." Turn then to one, most Sweet One, that face which once you turned away from holy David and as he was troubled, so shall I be consoled. Turn to me that face by which, before you turned it from him, you willed to increase his beauty. Let your right hand and your arm and the light of your countenance, which gained possession of the land for those fathers and mothers in whom you were well pleased, take possession also of my land. Indeed, I find nobody who speaks and treats so often and with such familiarity about your countenance and your face as David. And I cannot think that he lacked experience of it seeing that he calls for every judgment that he gives to issue from your face and looks for it to fill him full of joy. Moreover, when, declaring the blessedness of the people that can rejoice in you, he says: "They shall walk, O Lord, in the light of your countenance."

How much more purposefully can I walk, O God of my heart, when I keep looking to your face that it may guide my judgment, my conscience giving its full assent! I find then that your face, your countenance, means knowledge of your truth. For it is when your blessed people show you the face of good intentions that they rejoice greatly in the Holy Spirit and keep the feast of the great Year of Jubilee in contemplation and enjoyment of your truth. In the light of that truth, that face, they walk, directing all their goings and doings according to the judgments of your righteousness.

The knowledge of you has another face, another countenance. Moses was told concerning this: "You cannot see my face, for no person shall see me and live." It is to the sight and knowledge of the divine majesty that these words refer. That knowledge is best known in this life by unknowing. The highest knowledge that we can here and now attain consists in knowing in what way we do not know.

And yet, O Lord, though you have made the darkness of our ignorance and human blindness the secret place that hides your face from us, nevertheless your pavilion is round about you and some of your saints undoubtedly were full of light. They glowed and they gave light because they lived so close to your light and your fire. By word and example they kindled and enlightened others. They declared to us the solemn joy of this supreme knowledge of you for which we look hereafter when we shall see you as you are and face to face. Meanwhile, through them the lightnings of your truth have illumined the world and flashes have shone forth. These rejoice those whose eyes are sound although they trouble and perturb those who love darkness rather than light.

For this manifestation of your truth, through whomso-ever it comes, is like your sun that you make to shine on the just and the unjust alike. The sun, while ever retaining the purity of its own nature, nevertheless makes use of the substance of things as it finds them. It drys up mud and melts wax. It illumines every eye, whether sighted or blind, but with different effects. The seeing eye sees more when illumined, the blind continues in its blindness. So, too, it was when you, God's wisdom and Truth's light, by whom all things were made, came into the world. You enlightened every person coming into the world, but the darkness did not embrace you. But to as many as received you and the light of your truth, you gave the power to become sons and daughters of God.

Meditation Eight
The Passion of Christ

Through the healing power of Christ's Passion we are brought into the inner life of the Trinity.

O Righteousness supreme, do truth and mercy meet in you when the righteous humbly confesses according to the truth of human righteousness and the truth of your own righteousness as righteously has mercy on those that make this true confession. And when they thus proffer the kiss of a righteous confession you receive them with the kiss of peace. This is the mutual kiss of bridegroom and bride. That my face might merit to receive your kiss, O Lord, your face was spat upon. That my face might appear as fair and beautiful, your own was smitten by the hands of men and bruised with blows from rods. Your face was covered with dishonor in the eyes of all, that mine might be found beautiful and lovely in your sight. Moreover, you prepared for me the laver of your precious blood so that God's children might be washed in it. You bore fearful things for us. For we had done such fearful things that no face of repentance, no matter how great, could possibly atone for them before the face of utmost righteousness, had not your innocence been added to the things you suffered for our sake, had not you been yourself the Son whose plea was heard by reason of your godly fear.

For my hands, Lord, that did what they ought not, your hands were pierced with nails, your feet for my feet. For my unlawful use of sight and hearing your eyes and ears suffered the sleep of death. Your side was opened by the soldier's spear that through your wound out of my unclean heart might flow at last all that in the long process of disgrace had burned and penetrated into it. Lastly you died that I might live, and you were buried so that I might rise. This is the kiss your tenderness bestows upon your bride. This is your love's embrace for your beloved. Unhappy is the soul that has not shared this kiss! Unhappy too the soul that falls from this embrace! The thief's confession on the cross earned him this kiss. Peter received it when the Lord looked at him at the time of his denial and, going out, he wept most bitterly. And many of those who crucified you were turned to you after your passion and so united to you in this kiss. In the embrace from which the treacherous disciple fell, Mary, whom seven devils formerly possessed, rejoiced. In this embrace the publicans and sinners were enfolded, whose friend and fellow-guest you had become. It included Rahab, the converted harlot, Babylon that knows you, strangers, Tyre and the dark Ethiopians too. . . .

Those who kiss thus sweetly mingle their spirits and count it pleasure thus to share each other's sweetness. Receive, O Lord. Do not reject my whole spirit that I pour out on you in its entirety, despite the fact that it is altogether foul. Pour into me your wholly fragrant spirit that through your fragrance mine may stink no longer and the sweet smell of you, Most Sweet One, may permeate me ever more and more. This is what happens when we do what you told us to do in your remembrance. You could not have ordained a sweeter or a mightier means to forward the salvation of your sons and daughter. This is what happens when we eat and drink the deathless banquet of your body and your blood. As your clean beasts we there regurgitate the sweet things stored within our memory and chew them in our mouths like cud for the renewed and ceaseless work of our salvation. That done, we put away again in the same memory what you have done, what you have suffered for our sake. When you say to the longing soul: "Open your mouth wide and I will fill it," and we taste and see your sweetness in the great Sacrament that surpasses understanding, then we are made that which we eat, bone of your bone and flesh of your flesh. Thus is fulfilled the prayer that you made to your Father on the threshold of your passion. The Holy Spirit effects in us here by grace that unity which is by nature between the Father and yourself, his Son, from all eternity so that as you are one so likewise we may be made one in you. This, O Lord, is the face with which you meet the face of him who longs for you. This is the kiss of your mouth on the lips of your lover. And this is your love's answering embrace to your yearning bride who says: "My beloved is mine and I am his, he shall abide between my breasts." And again: "My heart has said: 'My face has sought you.'"

Meditation Eleven
Discernment ⚘

William shares his struggle in the process of discerning a more contemplative call and gives us some good norms for guidance.

I am groping in the noonday like a blind person now. In whatever direction I decide to move I go in fear of pitfalls and destruction. And like one blind I am told to go hither and thither by this way or by that, while I myself, just like a sightless person, do not know in what direction I am traveling nor by what road I go. Send out to me, O Lord, your light and truth. They have led and brought me to your holy hill and to your dwelling. "I am the way," you tell me, "by which you shall go. I am the truth to which you shall go. I am the life for whose sake you shall go. Whither to go you know, the way also you know." But I, Lord, do not know whither I am traveling, and how am I to know the

way. You have held me by my hand and led me in your will.
You held my hand when you stretched out yours to me.
Blind I was and crying after you with tears, and you said:
"Come unto me, all you who labor and are heavily laden
and I will refresh you."

Since I heard that, I have run the way of your commandments, for you have set my heart at liberty. I came to you,
O God, and I offered you my heart, my ready heart, saying:
"What will you have me to do?" And you replied: "Go, sell
all that you have and give it to the poor and come follow
me." I went. I ran. I sold all that I had, even my body and
soul. I gave nothing to the poor, because I possessed
nothing. I sold to you, O Lord, all that I had, and you are
my reward. You know that I have kept nothing for myself.
If there is anything that has escaped me and still lies hidden
in some secret corner of my conscience, I will search it out
and faithfully offer it to you. . . . (2-3)

Gather yourselves meanwhile, my soul and all my inward
parts. "The Word of God is living and effective. Sharper
than any two-edged sword, it pierces even to the dividing
asunder of soul and spirit and of the joints and marrow and
is a discerner of the thoughts and intents of the heart.
Neither is any creature unseen in his sight. All my concerns
are naked and open to his eyes.". . . (6)

Let us review our affections and actions. Let our affections be set on the center of truth, and thus the outward
action will correspond thereto as the circumference to the
center. Every affection is indeed owed to God. When he is
adhered to faithfully, wherever the circle of activity revolves
it cannot err from the right but meets itself truly, so that
its radius is of equal length at every point. There can be a
point without a circle but in no way can a circle be drawn
without a center point. (13)

The norm for action

Affection is sufficient if circumstances do not demand action or the possibility of acting is lacking. When the demands of love require action, true charity owes it to God and to the neighbor as the case may be. If necessity does not require it, the love of truth makes it our duty to hold ourselves at leisure for itself. As we always owe our entire affection to God, so also when we are at leisure we owe our whole activity to him. When a neighbor's need does not require it, we who divert a part of our affection or activity from God commit a sacrilege. But we whom necessity does require to act must not be so eager to do so that we fail to take stock of our own ability. The center of truth must be consulted as to whether we have the ability or not. If we have not and yet presume to act, we are not cleaving to the center and so we destroy the perfection of the circumference. For there are people who have no love for cleaving to the point of stability. They always want to be circling around the outside. . . . This is the norm: Let those from whom action is urgently demanded, if indeed it can be done, fix their attention on the truth and not refuse to do the act of service. If the truth when it has been consulted says they are unequal to the task and no fit person for it, then let them fix their soul in stillness on the stability of truth lest, being as it were on the rim of the wheel, they be sent over the precipice or error. . . . (13)

Spirit: I agree. This is indeed the marrow and the center of truth . . . (15)

Soul: That is how the matter stands. As once I took pleasure in being in authority so now my will is to be in subjection. And my self-will is glad to now have the excuse of my own needs; it does not allow me to attend to the needs of the brethren.

Spirit: Although, my soul, you do not lack a full compassion for the brethren's need, nevertheless your affection is even as you say. Nothing remains therefore but humble confession and striving after every virtue so that however unfruitful and useless we may appear outwardly we may not be found wholly barren and empty inside. And although the crowds bear down to silence us, let us cry with our whole heart and mind: "Jesus, Son of David, have mercy on me!" (16-17)

Meditation Twelve
The Spiritual Journey

Leaving our sins behind we make the journey to the promised land nourished by the bread of understanding and the water of wisdom.

"Hear my prayer, O Lord, give ear to my supplication in your truth. Hear me in your righteousness." Lord, you who are near to all who call on you in truth according to the promise made to us in the scripture of your truth. As the truth is present with you, my will is set to call on you in truth today. Hear me therefore, O Truth, in the multitude of your mercies and in the truth of your salvation. For I said: "Now I have begun. Be this your change, O right hand of the Highest." For my past sins and evils, which are great, inveterate and numberless, have made me vile and despicable to myself. As to my good qualities, if any such have been observed in me, I am most suspicious of them.

Therefore I come to you today as one whose whole past life is dead so that in you, O Fountain of life, I may begin again. If I have done any good things they are yours. To you I hand them over. Do return them to me in your own good time. The bad things that I have committed are my own. Alas, how many and how great they are, and most of them have slipped my memory. Oh, that a suitable repentance may efface them from your remembrance, too, the sins whose horror is such that no forgetfulness can ever wipe them out of my memory. I so detest their memory that I frequently wish I had completely forgotten all of them long ago. But please, Lord, do not you remember the transgressions of my youth. They were the Egyptian firstborn, whom you destroyed in Egypt. When I came out of Egypt, I left Egyptian deeds behind.

For a long time after that you led me through the wilderness and taught me and kept me as the apple of your eye. You rebuked me when I sinned. In my grief you gave me comfort. You instructed my ignorance until you brought me to the very threshold of the promised land. I stand there, beholding the delight of the land of the living that you show me. Then I remember what was told to Moses: "You shall see it, but you shall not enter it," and my whole being is convulsed with dread. If he deserved to hear those words for committing a single sin, what shall I hear who have today so many and such great transgressions to wipe out before you?

O Truth, all my past misdeeds, whether remembered or not, and all the chastisement which they merit, which is not past, are in your sight even when I say not a word. Let them come before your eyes today as I confess them to you. Let them be gathered in a single bundle to be burnt. It will be an enormous bundle, more than I can carry if there is no one to help me. I do not specify or make a list of them nor am I able to. But however much and in whatever way I have in truth sinned before you, O Truth, I own myself to be the sinner that you know that I am. Let nobody make light of my misdeeds to me nor yet exaggerate them. Let no one make them out as either less or more, not even myself. Before you, O God, I stand for trial. I will not spare myself, O Lord; you spare me.

Yet do not spare me in such a way as from this day to reckon me your enemy, to write bitter things against me and cause me to be brought to nought amid the sins of my past life. Keeper of men and women, do not any longer count me as your adversary, for being such has made me a grievous burden to myself. Rather take away the sin that comes between yourself and me. If you do pardon, Lord, then pardon me. If it pleases you to punish, then I myself will be your fellow-punisher. But do not bruise me with your blows as though you were my enemy, for I am ready to accept the scourge from you, and my grief shall be ever in your sight. I will tell out my iniquity and remember that I am suffering for my sin. For I am not handing myself over into the hands of an enemy. I am committing myself with complete trust into yours of which so often I have had experience. When one of your hands strikes me, the other one caresses. When one knocks me down, the other catches me so that I am not bruised. But there are times when, in an anger greater than that of enemies, you stretch out your hand, times when you turn your face away from us in wrath. Then you strike harder than an enemy, and then the heavens become as brass to us and the earth iron and everything is hard and everything is evil. For that is what always happens when our face is turned away. For your name's sake, O Lord, spare your servant in his. Flog us as much as you like, as long as the light of your face shines always upon us and you have mercy on us. Nevertheless you are the Lord of vengeance, remitting it or mitigating as you will. For you have turned our evils on yourself. Paying in your passion the things you did not take, you have prepared your throne for judgment so that, having been unjustly judged yourself, you may in justice absolve the justly judged.

Your judgments then shall help me, Lord. You shall look on me according to the judgment of those who love your name, even as you once passed judgment on the sinful woman who loved you, saying: "Her many sins are forgiven her for she loved much." May your own love be my advocate today in this my cause. If I shall have refused it on earth, I fear lest it may refuse me in heaven. If here I have been ashamed to own you, there you will be ashamed of me. I am ashamed—because my love is not what it ought to be. Because today is my judgment day, do you, Judge of my heart, judge me today also in this respect and sift my cause to see whether in fact I have the advocate I claim? For in this matter my spiritual sight is so darkened that I am entirely uncertain whether I see what I do not see or do not see what I do really see. Now most assuredly it seems to me that I always love your love insofar as I am moved by it whenever I think of it or am reminded of it. But when this does not happen, when I think of you or am reminded of you and am not moved or touched, I fear that perhaps this fact of my unmovedness convicts me of not always loving you—for the signs of your most present power and goodness strike and arouse the dullness of my perceptions everywhere and on every side.

O Light of Truth, dispel these shadows from me today and drive away the fog. Feed me with the bread of life and understanding and give me the water of wisdom to drink. Indeed, to understand your mysteries is both food and drink. They are the things we work at and labor over, taking them and as it were chewing them. Tough some of them, like drink, go through us as they are and refresh us in their own way. When we seek your love by means of understanding and sometimes find it, that is the very bread of life that strengthens the heart of men and women. This bread we often seek with great labor before we get it, for the penalty of Adam's sin is that we should eat our bread in the sweat of our face. But sometimes your Spirit blows where and when he will and breathes on us the favor of your love.

We hear his voice, because we receive the feeling of love. But we do not know by what judgment of your mercy it comes nor by what judgment of your justice it passes us by with only a greeting. Sometimes it comes with more sweetness, sometimes with more violence. This is drink. Feed me, O Lord, today with your bread that gives life to the world. With regard to these questions that I ask about your love, may a more firm and solid understanding be given me. And may the sweetness of your grace as a wholesome drink ready and soften this food lest a more solid food harm my feeble senses rather than strengthen them. . . . (1-7)

In the soul of your poor servant, Lord, your love is always present. But it is hidden like a fire in ashes until the Holy Spirit, who blows where he wills, is pleased to manifest it for our benefit the way and to the extent he wishes. Come, therefore, come, O Holy Love. Come, O Sacred Fire. Burn up the concupiscences of our reins and our hearts. As you will, hide your love to establish more abundantly the reign of humility in the face of your revealing flame. Manifest it when you will to manifest the glory of a good conscience and the riches it has in its house. Lord, to make me zealous to keep them, manifest those riches. Or, lest I be led rashly to squander them, hide them from me, until such time as he who has begun the good work in me shall also perfect it, he who lives and reigns through all the ages of ages. (18)

The Way of Faith

In his first Meditation William explored the vexing question of predestination: Why one is predestined and another is not. He wisely concluded with the answer he found in Augustine: Don't ask the question if you do not want to be in error. In a word, all rests with God in his freedom and love. Yet, again William, as he opens his treatise on faith, addresses himself to this fundamental mystery of faith. Why? Because it brings out our total dependence on God's mercy. He will have mercy on whom he will have mercy. And humility, the bedrock of all real relationship with God, demands we totally embrace the truth, that we fully accept reality—reality which proclaims that of ourselves we are nothing but sin, but of God we are the crown of creation, the very image of God, called to share divine life and happiness in a oneness with God that is beyond our comprehension. Faith with its accompanying humility is a sign of predestination, of the divine mercy in our lives.

Those who truly appreciate this gift of faith seek to nurture it in every way possible and to open themselves to the illuminating grace of the Holy Spirit, who leads us into true understanding and freedom. In the course of his *Mirror of Faith*, a book which William described as being "straightforward and easy," William gives not only clear teaching on just what faith is and its relation to charity and the rest of our life, but he also gives us some practical directives in regard to the temptations that assail our faith as well as the things which will aid us in walking in the way of faith. William also gives us here a very wholesome theology of sacramentality.

As one would expect in the spirituality of William, the way of faith leads to being fully integrated into the inner life of the Trinity by an affective union with the Holy Spirit, who is the communion of the Father and the Son. This is brought about by what William calls illuminating grace, a grace which brings faith beyond intellectual understanding to the intuitive experiential knowledge and understanding that comes from love-experience of the Beloved. This teaching of William present in all his writings is so consistent, clear and constant that we can only conclude that William is speaking from his own lived experience, experience that wholly colored and shaped his life and his outlook on life as a spiritual journey, a journey into God.

[handwritten: 2/3]

The Mirror of Faith

Among all the saving acts which our God, the God who saves us, has proposed to us to be observed for our salvation, these three—as the apostle Paul says—remain: faith, hope and charity. And they are to be observed in a special way by all who are to be saved. For in the mind of the faithful soul the Holy Trinity has constituted this trinity to their image and likeness. By this trinity we are renewed in the inner person in the image of the one who created us. This is the fabric of human salvation. All divinely inspired scripture looks to the building up and development of these in the hearts of the faithful.

We begin with faith. The apostle Paul does not deceive us when he says that during the time we pilgrimage far from the Lord, Christ dwells in our hearts by faith. Yet hope is also necessary for our journey. This it is that consoles us along the way. Take away from the traveler the hope of arriving and his courage to go on is broken. When we have arrived at where we are headed, faith will no longer exist. Will anyone ask us: Do you believe? No, indeed! For we will see God and contemplate him. Nor will hope be necessary when this comes about. For when someone possesses, what does he hope for? Yet faith and hope will not vanish but will pass over into their objects when what was believed will be seen and what was hoped for will be possessed. Charity will not only be present, it will be perfected, since what we love in this present life by believing in and hoping for we will then love by seeing and possessing. In the meanwhile, it is easy to see how really necessary are these three virtues for the person who desires to move toward that uncircumscribed light.

Three other things are also considered necessary: We must have eyes that serve us well so that we may look and see. Now the eye of the soul is the mind or reason, which needs to be pure and purged from all evil. At the beginning nothing but faith excels it. For if we do not believe that we will see what cannot as yet be shown to a sick soul (for only a healthy soul can see) we will make no effort to recover. But what if we believe we possess this faith, as I have said, and are able to see what can be seen, and still despair of being able to be healed? Are we not utterly casting ourselves out and contemning ourselves? Do we not follow the doctor's orders because as a sick person we feel these prescriptions are necessarily harsh? Consequently, hope must be added to faith.

What if we believe that we have all things and hope that we can be healed yet do not love that light which has been promised us? And what if we meanwhile believe that we ought to be content with the darkness which is now because of its familiarity usually agreeable to us? Aren't we spurning the physician? Therefore, a third thing is necessary: charity —and there is nothing so necessary! . . .

Since the upright live by faith, then these three virtues remain to form the life of the faithful. This is why infidels, who do not possess these three as do the faithful, do not follow a way of life comparable to that of the faithful. They believe other things, hope for other things; they love things other than do the faithful. And of necessity they live differently. Even if the use of certain things seems to be common to us and to them, we are still using these things very differently, for we orient their use to another goal. We thank God for these things in a different way, because we do not believe false and distorted things about God. And by not orienting these same things to the same goal but to the goal which God legitimately commands, we have the charity of a pure heart, a good conscience and a faith unfeigned. . . .

Perfection in this life is nothing other than forgetting entirely, by means of faith, hope and charity, those things that are behind and pushing on to those that are ahead, as the apostle Paul says, adding: "May as many as are perfect know this." All who truly seek the triune God must strive to have the trinity of these virtues in themselves and must eagerly study to conform themselves to what these virtues teach. Consciousness of them is a paradise of delights that enjoys an abundance of graces along with the pure delights of these holy virtues. Therein, as natives of this paradise, we converse with God. We often see God, often hear God speaking, often speak with God.

The Interdependence of Faith, Hope and Charity

Wherever these three cardinal virtues are, they are—like an image of the triune God—so joined and united to each other and among themselves that each one is in all, and all are in each one. Thus what, how much and the manner in which anyone of us believes, that and only that much and in that manner do we hope and love. May we hope for what we believe and love, and may we love what we believe and hope for. . . .

Faith must be sure so that hope may be sure and that charity may be sure. As no one of us can believe without hope, so none of us can hope unless faith is first present. So hope cannot take another form than does faith. The good that has been believed forms hope's longing, because the goodness that has been believed gives the believer the confidence to hope.

In the likeness of the Most Holy Trinity, therefore, faith

begets hope and charity proceeds from both, that is, from faith and hope, for we cannot help but love what we believe in and hope for. And in the same way what we love we also believe in and hope for. Just as in the Trinity the three persons are themselves co-eternal and consubstantial, so here too faith, hope and charity do not come before or after one another in time. . . .

There is one power for the three virtues of faith, hope and charity, for everything in this life is based on faith. By it we believe, we hope and we love what we do not see. This is faith, and we call it faith. By it we now walk as long as we pilgrimage to the Lord. . . . Although faith and hope will not pass away but will pass over into their objects, what we now believe in and hope for we will see and possess. To the extent that one is on pilgrimage through this life to the presence of the supreme truth . . . faith and hope are not so much conformed to charity as they are united to it. So it is that all three progress in unison in the light of the face of God, although the species of its own unique properties remains to each. Yet there often is or appears to be among these three only the single face of charity. To those who are climbing up from this vale of tears to the light of the promises from on high, this charity or esteem or love begins here at the stage of faith when that sun of justice arises continually for the person who is progressing for the first time out of the darkness of unbelief. For we begin not only to believe in and hope for what we do not see but also to love it to the extent that we believe and hope. Although the fullness or the perfection of this love will come to no one in this life, yet some progress in it must be hoped for until one finally arrives there where, for those who see face to face, will be the utter happiness of possessing what we loved, and our every virtue will be to love what we possess.

But meanwhile, faith is for those who walk, to rely upon it and to breathe to recover from the exhaustion of the journey and the weariness of the pilgrimage. The vision of the highest Good forever urges and draws every rational understanding toward the understanding and the love of itself. The closer we get to it, the purer we will be and the more eager to see what is promised to the pure of heart. This inspires everyone of us who strives to love the Lord our God with all our heart, with all our soul and with all our mind. We influence our neighbors in this as much as we can, for we love our neighbors as ourselves. But sometimes because of the sin of the first man and the punishments of his sin on the sons and daughters of his flesh, who are likewise sons and daughters of grace, there happens what the apostle Paul says of himself: "I am delighted with the law of God according to the inner person, but I see another law in my members warring against the law of my mind and making me a prisoner to the law of sin that is in my members." The flesh lusts against the spirit and the spirit against the flesh. As long as we are this way, it is clear to everyone that we do not love the Lord our God as we are obliged, namely with all that we are and with life itself. Frequently we desire very much and very carnally things beside God. As long as we live here, carnal yearning can be restrained and broken, but it cannot be so extinguished that it does not exist at all.

For this reason, although we are commanded in this life to have that perfect love which is unstinting and which, according to the precept of the law, we owe to the Lord God, no one entirely succeeds in reaching this love. It is commanded, all the same, lest we ignore the end toward which we must exert ourselves. . . .

Faith as a gift

We do not have a right faith about faith if we do not faithfully understand, above all, whose gift it is. Faith is of

free will, but of a will freed by grace. Our will held captive
under sin can never be free unless we are freed by him of
whom it is said: "If the Son shall free you, then you will be
truly free." By ourselves, we are free only to sin. By this
liberty all sin; everyone sins for the delight and love of
sinning. By this liberty the sons and daughters of justice
have been made the slaves of sin. They are incapable of
freely choosing or of perfecting any fruit of justice unless,
freed from sin by liberating grace, they are made servants
of justice. By justly deserting a person, a justice which is
deserved hardens whomever it wishes from among the
children of Adam who fall under the ancient damnation.
Mercy, which is not due, pities whomever it wishes by giving
help. Anyone who is helped offers a good and free will and
accepts faith; anyone who is deserted and forsaken poses
questions and deserves damnation. For scripture says:
"Why are they still asking questions? For who resists his
will?" A person who hopes, trembles; whereas one who
dares, despairs. The one is not asking the reason but
imploring mercy. Let the other who is forsaken, learn from
this what is deserved unless grace comes.

Faith implies humility and submission

Just as humility in the believer is the most certain sign of
a sheep of the Lord who shall be placed at his right hand,
so also the proud questioning of the unbelieving person is
a sign of the goat who will be placed at his left. For with
God none of us is saved unless we are humble in spirit. None
enters through the doorway of faith except with a bowed
head. The keyhole of the narrow gate is faith. A camel, a
person who is enormous and complicated, cannot go
through it unless shrunken and straightened to the humility
and simplicity of Christ. The proud and puffed up come to

the door of faith and, while they are being called to believe and to enter, they stand around disputing with the doorkeeper about why one has been admitted and another excluded until, by honest judgment of the doorkeeper, the door is slammed in their faces. And so, debating over those admitted and those excluded, they find themselves among those excluded. For they say about every last thing they do not grasp: This is a hard saying! They are harder! They turn their backs and go away. They are oriented to the things behind. But those poor in spirit — of such is the kingdom of heaven — working out their salvation with fear and trembling, not opening their mouths against heaven, come and plead. They pray to be admitted, and when they are admitted they worship, always trembling and forever in awe of the will of the potter who makes whatever he has wanted from his clay. Even having entered they are not secure as long as the senses of their flesh weigh them down. They catch fire with fear, go forward with love, burn to understand those things which they see, but they are afraid to scrutinize that which they should not scrutinize. Therefore, O creature, that you choose rightly and that you believe does not depend on the person willing and running but on God having mercy!

If you do not choose to believe, you do not believe. You believe if you choose to, but you do not choose unless you are first helped by grace. For none of us comes to the Son unless the Father draws us. How? By creating in us and inspiring in us a free will whereby we may freely choose that which we choose. This is so that what we choose rightly may be of our own will. By God's inspiration we make a voluntary assent of the mind to those things which concern God. What we believe in our heart leads to being right with God, what we confess by our mouth leads to salvation. And that is faith. Consequently it has been said: If you choose, you believe, but you do not choose to believe unless you are drawn by the Father. If you choose, you choose because you are drawn by the Father. So examine yourself, the apostle Paul says. If you are abiding in faith, prove yourselves to him. Do you not recognize that Christ is in you, unless in some way you are rejected? How is Christ Jesus in us? Through good will, of course, for peace comes to those of good will—which means by willing that Christ dwell in our hearts through faith. For this will is already to some extent the love of Christ, without which faith in Christ is utterly impossible. For devout faith cannot exist without hope and charity. . . .

Faith, which is submission to God's authority, needs love

Take an example from carnal affection with regard to God the Father. You believe on the authority of your elders something you learn from no experience. You believe without any doubt that you are the child of your father and mother. The authority of your father and mother, whom you believe, is so innate in you that you have no desire to refute it, because you love them. Nor can you, for in the judgment of someone who loves them, they deserve and seem worthy of being believed without hesitation. Embrace, then, the grace of divine adoption. You are the heir of God and the co-heir with Christ! Bend your knees to the Father of our Lord, Jesus Christ, from whom is named all fatherhood in heaven and on earth. May he, according to the riches of his glory, give you the power of being strengthened through his spirit in the interior person, of having Christ dwell through faith in your heart. Acknowledge the dignity of your race lest you prove yourself unworthy through unbelief. To deny our parents according to physical birth is a serious affront to nature. Acknowledge your mother:

grace. Bear patiently that she may nourish you in the womb of authority with the milk of simple history. And suckle at her breasts so that you may grow quickly. Grow! Go forward! To shrivel is to fail. Being born and growing up in a physical sense is not a matter of will, but spiritual birth and spiritual increase is a matter of will. In this the will is the child of grace. Grace begets this child, grace nurses, grace nourishes and carries this child along and leads the child all the way to perfection. That is until this child becomes like charity, a great and well-disposed will. By the working of charity, much kinder and more certain than any physical affection, the Holy Spirit is made present to bear witness to the children of grace that they are the children of God. . . .

Anyone of us who believes ought to know what we believe, who is the author of the doctrine, who is teaching it, that we may believe what we believe. Anyone of us who is really a faithful believer and of good will concerning the faith never picks out from among the matters of faith what we want to believe but without any retraction or hesitation we believe whatever divine authority has indicated must be believed. . . .

Faith and understanding

Humans are animals of weak wit and weaker faith. They do not perceive or scarcely perceive the things of God. The perception of faith is repugnant to human reason and human habits. Often people are not willing to believe, measuring the infinity of divine power by the infirmity of the human senses or of their own faith, as if (as human nature and its persuasions suggest) God were able to be or to do nothing except what we on our own appear able to understand about God. It is as if the sacraments of faith and the mysteries of holy scripture were human inventions. But those of faith and power, those who have been predestined to life, are anticipated by grace and like Paul attended by mercy that they may be faithful. Although occasionally they allow for their physical senses, in matters of faith they absolutely never let them gain the upper hand. As faithful servants of divine authority they subject themselves, completely applying their minds to the discipline of the faith which they have learned. They strive with all their devotion toward that which they have received: First to that which flesh and blood has revealed and then to that which no one but the Father in heaven reveals. First to the knowledge which night proclaims unto night, then to the word which the day utters to day. They are assiduous to learn not only what to believe but also to see things which fortify that faith against the enemies of faith. In this way faith may come to be where it does not exist and may be strengthened where it does exist. They so guide their life and even their habits that they may not only believe what is to be believed but may hope for and love it, that by loving they may understand and by understanding they may love. For in this way the spirit faithful to God deserves to receive the Holy Spirit. Grace merits grace, faith merits understanding. Devotion and the understanding of love lead every intellect back from captivity into the service of Christ so that the person who believes by loving may deserve to understand what he or she believes. As it is written: Unless you believe you will not understand.

Formerly, before faith came, we were guarded under the law, enclosed in that faith which was to be revealed. The law was our guardian in Christ Jesus so that by faith we might be made right with God. But now that faith has come we are not under a guardian but, having received the adoption of sons and daughters, we have been found children of God. We have received in our hearts the Spirit of

God by whom we cry: Abba, Father. So too in this time of grace, before the light of Christ's glorious gospels may begin to shine in our hearts, we have to be guarded and enclosed under the authority of that same gospel so that grace may be revealed in us at the time when God's mercy shall enlighten us. In the meantime, may authority be our guardian in Christ Jesus, so that through the humility of believing we may deserve to be enlightened by grace.

The Holy Spirit and illuminating grace

Once illuminating grace has come we are no longer under a guardian, for wherever the Spirit of the Lord is there is liberty. Having received the Spirit of the children of God, we ourselves are made the children of God both understanding and experiencing that we have God as a Father. When we have renounced all confidence in human authority, we may say to that Samaritan woman what her companions said to her: We no longer believe because of your word, for we ourselves have heard and we know that this is truly he, the Savior of the world. . . .

The temptations of doubt and understanding

If we forsake the guiding of authority at the beginning of our believing, we shall necessarily wander off the just way and walk according to the persuasions of our physical senses. Even some of the faithful stumble quite often. Although they do not stumble enough to fall, they are found to pass on not without some danger to life and detriment to their growth in faith. The fool says in his heart: There is no God. And someone else says: How does God know or is there knowledge in the Most High? They have doubts about the providence of God. Someone else wonders if for human salvation God ought to have been made a human. And there are many other things along this line. Even minds quite fervent in religion but still rather immature in the faith often undergo this kind of temptation about faith. These temptations come not by assailing them openly but by attacking them as if from the side and by plucking at the garment of faith from behind. They do not say: Yes, yes, no, no. But they whisper: Maybe, maybe. Maybe it is so, they say; maybe it is not. Maybe it is otherwise; maybe it is otherwise than written on account of something not written down. When the judgment of reason comes along, all doubts disperse and, although the garment of faith is found intact, it still feels plucked and battered.

In fact, there seems to be a reason that attacks and a reason that defends. The first one thinks about things in an animal and physical way. The other is spiritual and discerns all things spiritually. The one is, as it were, hesitant about unknown things. The other submits everything to authority. Moreover, it can hardly bear that any doubt should arise in any part of itself. It does not give a doubtful assent to anything coming from divine authority and from faith unfeigned. But what does a spirit do once it believes in God? It reads the gospels for itself, the words as well as the miracles of the Lord. And in all of them it venerates and adores the sacred vestiges of truth. When its faith is challenged, it says: You are the Christ, the Son of God. When its love is challenged, it says: You know that I love you and I lay down my life for you. And once we believe all matters of faith with an intrepid heart and are made right with God, let us confess with our lips to be saved as authority has declared. Nevertheless, if we cannot cut off from the ear of our hearts the "maybe so, maybe not" of murmuring temptation, we do not say this of ourselves but endure it with annoyance. . . . (11)

The apostle Paul says: It behooves those going to God to believe that God is a rewarder of those seeking him. Faith is the root of all the virtues and the foundation of all good works. Nor is there any virtue which is not derived from faith. There are no buildings but only ruins outside the foundation of faith. Because of this, the malice of the old serpent begins to infect this root first. He is always trying to shake this foundation first, if he can, so that faith will not even exist or, if it does, at least it will be imperfect so that any awareness of illuminating grace may be obscured. . . . (13)

We must not answer the spirit of blasphemy in any way or converse with him but only oppose to him the shield of faith. His virulent malice tries to pollute whatever we bring against him. He does not do this to get a satisfying answer but only to put on pressure to sadden the conscience of the believer or in some way to corrupt the purity of believer's faith. . . . (14)

Each vice must have its own antidote. The same remedy does not apply to all parts. What heals the head does not heal the foot nor can what heals the weakness of the soul heal the weakness of the flesh. Temptations of the flesh need affliction of the flesh and physical labors, but temptations of the soul cry out for the help of prayer, reading and meditation and any other spiritual undertaking there may be. One never acquires purity of faith except by true and profound humility of heart, dutiful devotion and unflagging perseverance in prayer. We must pray frequently, therefore, and say: Lord, increase our faith.

Often those who are advancing in faith, if they do not have the grace to forestall reason's challenges, suffer a natural uneasiness. Our rationality, in itself restless and impudent, often assaults faith with its reasoning even though it has no intention of contradicting it. It is seeking not to run against faith but to run with it. Human reason is used to acting in human affairs with a certain amount of belief. So it tries to act in the same way with divine realities. But since it mounts from a different direction, it slips, stumbles and slides down until it turns to the door of faith, to him who said: I am the door. Once it is humbled beneath the yoke of divine authority, the more humble it is the more securely does it enter in.

There are some persons who never experience temptations against faith: some because of the enormity of their laziness, some because of the torpor of their reason, some because of the certainty of enlightened faith.

The faith revealed by flesh and blood suffices for the dull-witted and the lazy. They are not tempted because they are not being examined spiritually. When we do not know what faith really is, the habit of assenting or a declaration of faith satisfies us. If we really knew what we were about we would certainly apply ourselves to understanding what we believe. The faith which flesh and blood reveals is one thing, another is that which is revealed by the Father who is in heaven. They are not identical. The faith is the same, the effect is different. The one teaches what we must believe, the other prompts an understanding of the faith. . . . The one is the teacher, the guardian of human infirmities, the other is itself the inheritance and perfection of liberty. The one tolerates lazy persons nor does it exclude dull-witted persons, holding out to everyone the lines of truth. The other receives only those who are fervent in spirit, serving the Lord and having the eyes of their heart enligtened. (15-16)

The faith of the simple

We are not calling dull-witted those simple sons and daughters of God with whom God has frequent communication. Their unique merit and singular grace is that they deserve to receive the faith by God's revelation—not just the faith which flesh and blood reveals but that which comes from the Father who is in heaven. Those who are taught by God learn from the Holy Spirit apart from the racket of argumentative words and reflections. (If the Spirit himself is not present in the teacher and disciple in this kind of teaching, the noisy reasonings of reason fail.) These are not lazy persons, they are simple and uniquely strong and prudent in faith. Nor in their silence are they to be considered dull-witted; rather they are wise in what they have "unwisely" accepted because they have sensed the Lord in goodness. They sense with a sense of love whatever they believe about God. They savor what they sense, and when reasonings tire and drop out they keep going, for they walk simply, they walk confidently. For they trust not in the chariots of their own cleverness or in the horses of human self-reliance but in the name of the Lord, not in book learning but only in the power of the Lord and in his justice. For they make no distinction in faith. They analyze nothing. Continually offering every judgment of their own reason to be enlightened by the Holy Spirit and directing their every sense to assent in faith, they sweetly and confidently seize its spiritual fruit. And they sense something of the Lord in his goodness, for they seek him in simplicity of heart. And he is found by them, for they do not tempt him. He appears to them because they have faith in him. There is fulfilled in them what the Lord Jesus, praying to the Father for the disciples, said: "And truly these have known that I have come forth from you." How have they known? He continues: ". . . and they have believed that you sent me." Yes, they have really known, for they have really believed.

By no means are we extolling the simple person simply believing as if to discredit a person of spiritual discernment, someone who while a scrutinizer of majesty is yet an admirer of piety and imitator of simplicity. Not only do such persons evade the enticing snares of temptation but, learning from temptations, they progress magnificently. Their graces are different.

It is one thing to have simple faith and to grasp the sweetness of its fruit in the heart. It is another thing to understand what one believes and always be prepared to render a reason for one's faith.

Simple faith savors but gives no light and is more removed from temptations. The other type, although it is savored only with effort, it gives light and is safer against temptations. While we advance step by step in the faith, with Christ dwelling within our hearts by faith, we possess a sure knowledge of the various matters of faith. We foster the faith which flesh and blood reveals to us with a very fervent embrace. And when it is given to us, we rest sweetly in what our Father who is in heaven reveals. And although we are often overtaken by the simple who are using the shortcut of their devout simplicity, we are nevertheless not held back from the fountain of grace, which is open to all. Working in sorrow in the thorns and nettles of our earth, amid the temptations of our corrupt nature, by the sweat of our brows ever since Adam's curse, we eat our own bread. Sometimes, although we do not know it, we, like Jacob, find the blessings of the Lord in the meadow of our hearts. For the effort of spiritual exertion, expended faithfully in faith, cannot be useless nor can the sorrow of this time be cheated of its reward. Illuminating grace is often present to a struggling faith and brings to it, as if by the thrust of a lance, a recognition of and hope for things invisible. And in that recognition and hope it brings love. Without any delay the love coming from faith by the mediation of hope continuously rises.

Do not fear, servant of God. Do not run about, do not

waste your steps. Infidels seek signs, the hesitant need wisdom. Embrace Christ crucified, a stumbling block to those predestined to ruin, foolishness to those who are wise in their own eyes, but to those who are called and justified, the wisdom of God and the power of God. For the foolishness of God is wiser and his weakness stronger than all. If you consult the experience of faith, it seems foolish and weak. Yet if, with the apostle Paul, you have the mind of Christ, you will understand that the Word of God is supreme wisdom. The foolishness of this wisdom is the flesh of the Word. This is so that those who are carnal, who are not able through the prudence of the flesh to attain to the wisdom of God, may be healed through the foolishness of preaching and the simplicity of faith. Be foolish that you may be wise, and there will be revealed to you the plan hidden from all ages in God, who created every creature. Be as weak as God's weakness, and you will learn how exceedingly great is the greatness of his power in those of us who have believed by his power.

Momentary and passing confusion over what they believe should not frighten the faithful. This is no lack of good conscience with regard to the faith nor a lack of the presence of the Holy Spirit, even if this occurs during an examination for martyrdom. O faithful ones, nature in its innocence does not damn you; it boggles at the unfamiliar. It does not draw away from the faith but draws back in reflection. Sometimes it simply believes, but sometimes it seeks to know. Consider the mother of the Lord, an outstanding witness to faith. Once she had received the good news of our salvation and of her conception by the Holy Spirit, she believed with absolute certainty that she would be the mother of the Lord. Nonetheless, there was something she needed to know: the way in which this mystery would be fulfilled. She asked: How shall this be, for I do not know man? She held the reality by faith, but she wanted to know the manner. Her faithful soul embraced the reality, made strong by the grace of which she was full. But her nature, astonished, was wondering how it would happen. She was already sensing within herself the Holy Spirit operating in a unique way. But she did not know how the Spirit would accomplish in her flesh without the help of flesh the wonderful things she believed. The angel said to her: "The Spirit of the Most High will come upon you, and the power of the Most High will overshadow you." It is as if he said: The finger of God is here. So, too, concerning the spiritual regeneration of baptism, the Lord replied to Nicodemus, who wanted to know the manner of regeneration: "The Spirit breathes where he wills and you hear his voice and you know not where he comes from and where he goes. Thus is everyone who is born of the Spirit." To those fretting about the sacramental mystery of his body and blood, Jesus says: "It is the Spirit who gives life, the flesh does not profit anyone." For one and the same Spirit does all this as he wills, so constituting the sacraments of faith that some of them are the corporal and visible signs of the sacred reality—as in baptism and in the sacrament of the body and blood of the Lord—and others are only sacred things concealed and open to investigation by a spiritual understanding guided by Holy Spirit himself. Of these last the apostle Paul says: "That he might make known to you the mystery of his will." (16-19)

Faith in the sacraments and mysteries of religion

The will of God is the hidden and highest mystery of all the sacraments, which he makes known according to his good pleasure to whom he chooses and as he chooses. It is a mystery which, because it is divine, in some divine manner he reveals to the one who is worthy in the process of making that person worthy. Better yet, it is not divine, it is God, for it is the Holy Spirit who is the substantial will of God. This is the will of God whereby God makes all that he wills. About it it is written: "Everything that the Lord willed he did." The same Holy Spirit, then, makes himself known to the person into whom he pours himself. The very will of God makes himself known to the person in whom it is accomplished. Nor is the will known anywhere other than where the Spirit is. Even if the eye of human reason cannot hide itself from the brightness of his light and truth, only the person who does his will can be a partaker of his sweetness. And only by willing what God wills.

Just as there are many persons who have a soul and do not know what a soul is, so there are many who have grace but do not know what it is. To the person on whom it exerts an influence, grace reveals the external sacraments when the very reality signified in all the sacraments is working within. It is the Holy Spirit himself who sanctifies externals so that they may be the sacraments of so great a reality. By revealing them, he commends them to the faithful conscience in whom the hidden grace effects the reality of the sacrament. God is more intimate to us than our inmost being. For our outer being, for the senses of the body, God establishes the external sacraments through which he would lead our inmost being to his inmost being. Through the workings of the physical sacraments he gradually excites in us spiritual grace. It is for this purpose that he humbled himself to fellowship with our humanity: that he might make us partakers of his divinity.

As the Author of our salvation had commanded, therefore, our flesh is washed outwardly in the waters of baptism; inwardly the soul is purified by the operation of the Holy Spirit. And thus justified in the faith of the Son of Mary and the Son of God, sinners are made the sons and daughters of God. The faithful eat physically but incorruptibly the physical but incorruptible food of the body and blood of the Lord. . . . We eat what conforms us to God through the understanding of reason; through enlightened love we eat what unites us to God. Accustomed to temporal things we must be cleansed by temporal things. And once cleansed, we shall not be worthy of contemplation of the eternal unless, in the process of being purified by temporal things, we have summoned forth faith. These things are indeed temporal and transitory, but through the first fruits of the Spirit they nevertheless bear the first fruits of things eternal. This is most compellingly present to us in the person of the Mediator who, remaining himself eternal God, has been made man in time that through him, temporal and eternal, we may pass from things temporal to the eternal. Consequently, as I have said, we eat the body of the Lord and drink his blood physically, but we are refreshed spiritually. The assent of our faith has been taught step by step by these foundations of Christian piety. . . .

First of all, then, we are obliged to give a simple and pure assent of faith to the realities of God without any wavering or hesitation. Then, to understand what we believe, along with observing and obeying the commands of God, we are obliged to confide to the Holy Spirit all our spirit and understanding. This is not so much an undertaking of reason as the affection of simple and devout love. And so, by the serious application of an absolutely humble piety rather than by the power of our ingenuity, we shall deserve to have Jesus begin to entrust himself to us. With grace illuminating the understanding of our reason, the assent of faith will be changed into the instinct of love to recognize inwardly the sacrament of the will of God. . . .

Placed in the body, we have been limited to the corporeal forms of the sacraments and to obedience to the wisdom of God who instituted them. We are confronted with the physical forms of the corporal sacraments, and we are called by their external signification to their inner grace, to the inner dimension they signify. We are sickly, languishing from the corruption of nature. We ought to want to be made healthy. Our sickness is a product of the changeableness of our mortal nature. Faith in our Mediator is the medicine which carries us from here to there. Faith pertains especially to those things accomplished for us in time. By it our hearts are cleansed so that they may be made capable not merely of believing but of understanding the realities of eternity. If in faith we act faithfully then belief deserves truth and changeableness passes to the unchangeable eternity of the realities believed. As long as we are being purified let us give the sacraments of these realities their due reverence, that is, faith in those very realities. Then, purified and helped by them, we may advance toward the reality which those acts have accomplished and their sacraments now accomplish, and our faith may advance to the contemplation of eternal realities.

Proper dispositions for faith

The unclean soul, the impure conscience, the proud mind, and curious conceit are rightly kept at a distance from the quest of the divine sacraments and mysteries. For the spirit of discernment flees anything false and will not dwell in a body subject to sin. Wisdom will not enter into an ill-disposed soul. But humble piety, believing love and a pure conscience, the simplicity of the child of God and the poor in spirit, although these reverently withdraw, they are called forward by Holy Spirit. In a special sort of way they are drawn to inquire into things divine. For they love and therefore they seek, and when they do seek they seek to love still more. Consequently, O faithful soul, when in your faith the more hidden mysteries impinge on your timorous nature, be brave and say, not to stave them off but to follow them: How can these things be? Let your question be your prayer. Let it be your love and your humble desire, not considering the majesty of God in lofty matters but seeking salvation in the saving acts of the God of our salvation. And the Angel of Mighty Council will reply to you: When the Paraclete shall come whom I will send to you from the Father, he will bear witness of me and will bring all things to your mind. The Spirit of truth will teach you all truth. As no one knows those things that are of humans except the spirit which is in them, so no one knows those things of God except the Spirit of God. Hasten to be partakers of Holy Spirit then. He is present when he is invoked, and he will not help unless he is invoked. When invoked, he comes. He comes in the abundance of God's blessing. He is the torrent of the river making happy the city of God. And if, when he shall come, he finds you humble and quiet and fearing the words of God, he will rest upon you, and he will reveal to you what God the Father withholds from the wise and prudent of this world. Those things which Wisdom was able to teach the disciples on earth will begin to enlighten you. But they could not bear to hear them until the Spirit of Truth came, who taught them all truth. In such perceiving or learning, it is futile to expect from the mouth of an human what could not be perceived or learned from the tongue of Truth himself. For as Truth himself has said: "God is spirit."

And just as it is necessary that those who worship him worship him in spirit and in truth, so it behooves those wanting to know and understand him to seek the understanding of faith, the sense of pure and undivided truth, only in the Holy Spirit. For in the darkness and ignorance of this life he is the light that enlightens the poor in spirit. He is the purity that draws them. He is the sweetness that entices them, he is our access to God. He is the love of the

lover, he is devotion, he is piety. He reveals to the faithful
from faith in faith the justice of God, because he gives grace
for grace and to the faith of the hearer, the faith that
enlightens. . . .

The proper object of faith

Unhesitatingly believe that the Holy Trinity, Father, Son
and Holy Spirit, are of one substance and have, with an
inseparable equality, a divine unity; that there are not three
gods but one God. Believe that God was made man for us
as the best medicine to heal the tumor of our pride. He is
the profound sacrament for our redemption and the forgive-
ness of our sins. He has performed miracles and has risen
from the dead. . . . Reflect on what the Divine, humbling
himself, has brought about in the world. Be attentive to the
Lord in his goodness. How becoming to God was this
activity. First, in the cause of human salvation the Father
did not spare his Son nor did his Son spare himself. In the
Son the supreme good was manifested in the world. He
taught us how to love God as he ought to be loved. Loving
us to the extent even of giving himself, he taught us how to
love God at the cost of ourselves—we, poor wretches, who
only knew how to love ourselves even to the contempt of
God. This is piety. This the proper adoration of God by
which God ought to be adored by his creature. This is the
wisdom which the Supreme Wisdom brings into the world,
creating in it so many glorious martyrs, so many persons
who achieve perfection by putting themselves and the world
at naught. This is the wisdom that belongs to God and the
person who has the mind of God, to the one who lives by
the spirit of Christ's life to the point of sensing his love,
who loves to the point of imitating his likeness. . . . In our
Mediator there shines forth in a unique way that long-

established definition of wisdom: That understanding of
things human and divine that enables one to imitate our
Lord Jesus Christ who, although he was in the form of God
and did not think it robbery to make himself equal to God,
humbled himself, taking the form of a slave even to the
point of dying on the cross. Who, what, for whom did he
do this?

In remembering, understanding and loving we are made
similar to the Supreme Wisdom and become wise in God.
We show this wisdom by adoring God as God. By this
adoration we season our lives, our manner of acting and our
actions and everything else with a sort of divine savor, which
affects all who behold us. It anoints them with a kind of oil
of gladdening grace so that, seeing our good works, they
glorify our Father in heaven. We are gracious toward our
friends, patient and kind toward our enemies. We can be
kind to anyone we want to. We are well-disposed to all. And
we hold to that natural law: Do not do to another what you
do not want done to yourself, but insofar as you can, do to
everyone else what you want done to yourself.

Various aids to faith

If only everyone who professes this faith would live it to
the full! May everyone who has it glory in being numbered
among the ranks of the faithful. No one should hold that
one can have this faith toward God who is still keeping faith
with the world. For this reason the apostle Paul says: Those
who thrust off a good conscience have made shipwreck of
their faith. A bad conscience easily suffers the shipwreck of
its faith. Those whose mind is corrupted by a yearning for
the world and the flesh conduct themselves neither honestly
nor honorably in regard to faith. . . . As the serpent's prudence accustoms it to expose its whole body to protect its

head in which its life is contained so the faithful refuse to do or to suffer nothing as long as the health of their faith remains intact.

We must therefore assiduously pray to our Father in heaven that if he allow our faith to be tested by being led into temptation he will not allow it to suffer temptation to the point of being overcome. Rather may he offer with the temptation the growth we need to sustain it. We must seek the help of grace very seriously, with great devotion, standing against the impulses of the flesh and the passion of our nature, lest our faith fail. May it instead bear fruit in patience until, little by little, the grace of the Holy Spirit lifts up our whole being to a perfect faith. . . . In order to build up our faith, to confirm our hearts, and to enlighten our awareness in faith, let us prudently look to those great lights of the Church, the men and women of great spiritual knowledge, wisdom, and proven holiness, and to their teaching and writings, their works and martyrdoms. Let us say to ourselves against the movements of our own temptations: Are you really better than they are, holier, wiser, sharper, than those who have taught the world what they have learned from the Lord? They preached it magnificently. They have handed it down to us in rich descriptions. They have confirmed it by their lives and miracles and have made it holy by their deaths and martyrdoms. . . .

No person in his or her right mind is so depraved that he or she does not know that God is the creator of every creature. God is above every creature in that every creature comes from him. He is beyond all time, for with him there is no time. He is beyond all place, for with him there is no place. He, the changeless one, changes all things; immovable, he moves all things. The source of all things, of all change and all motion, he yet must be seen as the immovable power and rational cause of all things created and moved. . . . (25)

Bk 2/3 ☩☿

The goal of the life of faith

When we, thirsting for the living God, look at the glory
of God, then led by grace we encounter the Mediator
between God and us, the God-man Jesus Christ, the image
of the invisible God. Because of the magnitude of the
goodness whereby he was made human for us and because
of the power of the majesty whereby he is God, we experience in ourselves the splendor of God's grace. We become
what the apostle Paul calls the figure of his substance. Paul
says: "We, looking at the glory of God with face unveiled,
are transformed into that same image from glory to glory
as by the Spirit of the Lord." We love and our love is the
sense whereby we experience him whom we experience. And
we are somehow transformed into what we experience, for
we do not experience him unless we are transformed into
him, that is, unless he is in us and we in him.

amen ☩

As the outer senses of the body concern themselves with
bodily things so does the inner sense with inward realities,
that is, with rational and divine or spiritual things. But the
inward sense of the soul is understanding. Yet, a greater and
worthier sense and the source of a purer understanding on
the part of the soul is love if love is pure. For by this sense
the Creator himself is experienced by the creature. By this
experience the Creator is understood insofar as God can be
experienced or understood by a creature. Our soul when it
seeks to experience is by this experience changed into what
it experiences. . . . In those things which pertain to God, the
sense of the mind is love. By this it experiences whatever it
experiences of God according to the Spirit of life. And the
Spirit of life is the Holy Spirit. By him anyone loves who
loves what truly ought to be loved.

Nothing is loved unless it is good or is thought to be good.
So it is understood that every love and all love is due only
to the supreme good. Love always returns to the supreme

good if it is not held bound or captive elsewhere where it is deceived by a false good.

The love of God is to our love, to our natural affection, what our soul is to its body. If the soul is in it, the body is alive. If the soul is not in it, then the body is a carcass and does not sense what it ought to be sensing. When we are alive and sense through love what ought to be sensed, we are transformed into what we experience. We are made one spirit with God to whom we are attached. . . .

This process happens in a more forceful and more worthy manner when the Holy Spirit who is the substantial will of the Father and Son attaches our will to himself. Then we love God and by loving experience him. Then the will is unexpectedly and entirely transformed, not into the nature of the divinity certainly, but into a kind of blessedness. This is something beyond the human form yet short of divinity. It is found in the joy of illuminating grace and the experience of an enlightened conscience. Now the human spirit, which before had scarcely been able to say in the Holy Spirit: Jesus is Lord, now in the midst of the children of adoption cries out: *Abba*, Father! And not only our spirit but also our flesh, experiencing already the first fruits of the promised incorruption and glorification, will renounce itself joyfully, and swiftly run after its spirit as the spirit does after God. This is the rejoicing of a blessed people knowing jubilation, walking in the light of God's countenance, exulting in his name, a people to whom the righteousness of being raised up is God and he himself is the glory of their power. For this is the taking on of the Lord, our holy king of Israel. When we experience in goodness him who has been made like unto us we experience in ourselves what also is in Christ Jesus our Lord. For we are made like unto him by suffering joyfully with him now. Afterward we shall be like to him by reigning with him. (26-30)

The presence of the Holy Spirit

Over the impoverished and needy love of the poor in spirit and over what they love, the Holy Spirit, the love of God, caringly hovers. That is, he performs his works in them. This he does not through the compulsion of any need but through the abundance of his grace and generosity. This was signified when he hovered over the waters—whatever those waters may have been. The sun hovers over the waters, warming and lighting them and drawing them to itself by its heat, by some natural force, that it may thereby furnish rain to a thirsty earth in the time and place of God's mercy. Just so the Love of God hovers over his faithful, breathing upon them and enriching them. He clasps to himself those who by a sort of natural impulse, like fire leaping up, seek him. He unites them to himself so that the spirit of those who believe, having trusted in God, may be made one with him.

The Father and the Son are equally called spirit; for God is spirit. It is also proper for the Holy Spirit to be called by this same word in a particular way, though he seems not so much the spirit of each as their communality. The Holy Spirit himself communicates to us this "spirit" so that, as the apostle Paul says, we may be made one spirit with God both in name and in reality. It is not just one person but many who have one heart and one soul in the Spirit by sharing in this supreme charity at the source of which is the unity of the Trinity. (32)

Union with God

Such is the astounding generosity of the Creator to the creature, the great grace, the incomprehensible goodness, along with the devout confidence of the creature for the

Creator, the responsiveness, the tenderness of conscience, that somehow we find ourselves in the midst of the embrace and the kiss of the Father and Son, that is in the Holy Spirit. And we are united to God by the charity whereby the Father and Son are one. We are made holy in him who is the holiness of both. The sense of this good and the tender love of this experience, as great as it can be in this miserable and deceptive life, although it is not now full, blesses us with a true and truly blessed life! In the future it will be a full and fully blessed life, unchangeably eternal. As Paul put it: "When we know as we are known, when what is in part will have been done away with and what is perfect will have come, then God will be seen as he is." It is dangerous presumption to look for the fullness of this knowledge in this life. Just as unbelief concerning what should be believed is to be avoided, so is rashness concerning what is to be understood. For the time being authority governs faith, truth governs understanding. For the time being, although God cannot be seen or recognized as he is, it helps us no little bit if we accept nothing in God's place which is not God himself, if our mind shuts out and rejects anything physical or localized which occurs to it or anything which would be seen as a quality or quantity. Let the mind reflect on truth itself insofar as it can, and let it know it with absolute certitude and love it. . . . This truth is God, who is what he is and from whom and through whom and in whom is all that is. He is that supreme good from whom and in whom and through whom all that is good is good.

We should always yearn to taste, insofar as it may be granted us, how sweet the Lord is. When the devout mind, the humble mind, does not deserve to be admitted into that purity on account of its own impurity — or when, if it is admitted to taste it, it is not able to enjoy it because of its lack of hunger — let it be driven out, not without sighs of love and tears of sorrow. Let it embrace the goodness and discipline of the Lord: goodness because what is unworthy is admitted there and discipline because what is cast out is thereby taught. And let it bear this patiently as long as it is being cleansed. Let it make itself more worthy to be admitted more frequently and to stay longer. . . .

God's face revealing itself to the person who loves is his will. His face is the knowledge of his truth. Nor do we ever really experience God unless God is formed in us by this face or unless our love, as ones experiencing God, is conformed to his face. Nor do we judge well in our love unless our judgment comes out of the experience of that countenance. Nor is anything done well nor does anyone ever live well unless the actions and the life of the person willing to live according to God are formed thereby. Neither is anything sought in the light of that countenance except by a gift of grace which anticipates all our deserving. (33)

Concluding prayer

O you whom no one truly seeks and does not find, find us that we may find you! Come in us that we may go to you and live in you, for surely this comes not from the person willing nor from the person running but from you who have mercy. Inspire us that we may believe. Strengthen us that we may hope. Call us forth and set us on fire that we may love. May everything of ours be yours that we may truly be in you, in whom we live and move and have our being. (33)

A Summing Up

In what was to prove to be the last years of his life, William spent a time of refreshing retreat among the Carthusians of Mont Dieu, not far from his own Signy. The monks there showed a great interest in his writings, and on his return to Signy he sent them copies of many of his writings. It is thanks to this that we have the sole manuscript of some of these writings. In addition, William took the opportunity to show his gratitude and serve the novices there by writing a letter which has rightly been called "The Golden Epistle." It is an insightful and well-worked-out, concise summary of his basic teaching on the spiritual journey.

After briefly and clearly describing three states of spiritual growth—which he calls the animal state, the rational state and the spiritual state—and their respective stages of progress, William goes on to explore each in practical detail. Since this summary is placed in the context of a letter which is addressed primarily to the novices, this provides an excuse for dwelling at greater length on the first state, the animal state. This in fact reflects William's life-long primary concern for the young, the beginners, among whom he ever humbly placed himself. William's section on the last state, the spiritual state, seems disproportionately short. The fact is that those in this state need little instruction. They are guided in all by the Holy Spirit himself. This stage is set before the young to encourage them, giving them a glimpse of what to expect, a deification beyond description, more than any human can really desire.

In his rather lengthy introduction to this Letter to the Brothers of Mont Dieu, William draws upon the gospel scene dear to contemplatives, the theophany atop Mount Tabor, to offer a salutary warning. We must take care not to turn even the holiest of occupations into a selfish and self-centered project. The only way we can come into union with God is through love. And love is of its very nature self-giving. My first spiritual father put it another way: Beware of seeking the consolations of God rather than the God of consolation.

We find in this remarkable treatise written in the last years of William's life, many of the themes that were very present in his earlier writings, such as seeking the face of God and its realization in unity of spirit. Here they arc skillfully placed in a carefully constructed scheme rich in psychological insight. Solitude is emphasized in one section because William is writing in first place to Carthusians, but what he says is readily adaptable to every Christian life. Although William traces the way to the highest and most intimate union with the Divine in the Trinity, he nonetheless retains a deep devotion to our Lord in his humanity. Note especially his understanding and appreciation of spiritual communion.

The Golden Epistle

When those who were with him on the holy mount had seen the glory of the Lord's Transfiguration, Peter at once was rapt out of himself and did not know what he was saying, for the sight of our Lord's majesty inspired him with the wish to subordinate the common good to his own personal enjoyment. Yet he was in full possession of his senses and well aware what he was saying inasmuch as the taste of the sweetness made him judge that it was best for him to remain in that state always. So he expressed his desire for this life in the fellowship of our Lord and the citizens of heaven whom he had seen with the Lord: "Lord, it is good for us to be here always. Let us make here three booths, one for you, one for Moses and one for Elijah." If this request of his had been granted he would doubtless have made three other booths, one for himself, one for James and one for John.

After our Lord's passion, while the memory of the blood he had shed for them was still fresh and warm in the hearts of the faithful, the deserts were filled with men and women who had taken up the solitary life, embraced poverty of spirit and rivaled one another in spiritual exercises and the contemplation of God, seeking a leisure that would yield rich fruit. Among them we read of those Pauls, Macarii, Antony, Arsenius and so many other leading figures in the commonwealth of this holy way of life, outstanding names in the City of God. They are honored with triumphant titles of nobility that were won by victories over the world and the prince of this world and over their own body, won by cultivating their souls and worshiping God. . . .

It is for others to serve God, it is for you to cling to him; it is for others to believe in God, know him, love him and serve him; it is for you to taste him, understand him, be acquainted with him, enjoy him. This is no slight matter, no easy goal. But he who, in his love, makes you such promises is almighty and good. He will be faithful in fulfilling them and untiring in giving help. To those who in their great love for him pledge themselves to great things and, believing and trusting in his grace, undertake what is beyond their own strength, he imparts both the will and the desire. And he follows up by bestowing also the power to achieve. Let the calumniators calumniate as they will; if you faithfully do what is humanly possible for you to do, God himself in his mercy will give judgment for his poor one, will champion your cause because you did what you could. . . .

To "seek the face of God" is to seek knowledge of him face to face, as Jacob did. It is of this knowledge, the apostle Paul says: Then I shall know as I am known. Now we see a confused reflection in a mirror, but then we shall see face to face. We shall see him as he is. Always to seek God's face in this life by keeping the hands unstained and the heart clean is that piety which, as Job says, is the worship of God. Those who lack it have received their souls in vain, that is to say, they live to no purpose or do not live at all, since they do not live the life to live which they receive their souls.

This piety is the continual remembrance of God, an unceasing effort of the mind to know him, an unwearied concern of the affections to love him. This way, I will not say every day, but every hour finds the servant of God occupied in the labor of ascesis and the effort to make progress or in the sweetness of experience and the joy of fruition. This is the piety concerning which the apostle Paul exhorts his beloved disciple in the words: "Train yourself to grow up in piety. For training of the body avails for little while piety is all-availing since it promises well both for this life and for the next. . . ."

Those who have God with them are never less alone than when they are alone. It is then that they have undisturbed fruition of their joy. It is then that they are their own master and are free to enjoy God in themselves and themselves in God. It is then that in the light of truth and the serenity of a clean heart a pure soul stands revealed to itself without effort, and the memory enlivened by God freely pours itself out in itself. Then either the mind is enlightened and the will enjoys its good or human frailty freely weeps over its shortcomings. . . .

From all perfection is demanded, although not the same kind from each. If you are beginning begin perfectly, if you are already making progress be perfect in doing that. If you have already achieved some measure of perfection, measure yourself by yourself and say with the apostle Paul: "Not that I have already won the prize, already reached fulfillment. I only press on in the hope of taking possession of it, as Christ Jesus has taken possession of me. This at least I do: forgetting what I have left behind, intent on what lies before me, I press on with the goal in view, eager for the prize: God's heavenly summons in Christ Jesus."

Then he adds: All of us who are perfect must be of this mind. Clearly the apostle's teaching in this passage is that the perfection of the just in this life consists in wholly forgetting what lies behind and pressing on with might and main to what lies before. And the place where the perfection of this perfection will be achieved is where the prize of God's heavenly summons will be grasped with full security. . . .

The three states

As one star differs from another in brightness, so cell differs from cell in its way of life: There are beginners, those who are making progress, and the perfect. The state of beginners may be called "animal"; the state of those who are making progress, "rational"; and the state of the perfect, "spiritual." Those who are still animal may on occasion claim forbearance in some respects in which no indulgence should be shown to those who are considered as already rational. Again certain things are tolerated in the rational which are not tolerated in the spiritual. Everything in them must be perfect, calling for imitation and praise rather than for blame. . . . As each is marked by a name proper to it, so each is recognized by distinctive pursuits. All those who are born of the light should consider carefully in the light of the present day what is lacking to them, whence they have come, how far they have come, the progress of the day and the hour.

There are the animals who of themselves are not governed by reason nor led by affection, yet stimulated by authority or inspired by teaching or animated by good example they acquiesce in the good where they find it. Like the blind, led by the hand they follow, that is, imitate others. Then there are the rational, whom the judgment of their reason and the discernment that comes of natural learning endows with knowledge of the good and the desire for it, but as yet they are without love. There are also the perfect, who are led by the spirit and are more abundantly enlightened by the Holy Spirit. Because they relish the good which draws them on, they are called wise. They are also called spiritual, because the Holy Spirit dwells in them, as of old he dwelt in Gideon.

The first state is concerned with the body, the second with the soul, the third finds rest only in God. Each of them makes progress after its own fashion, and each of them has a certain measure of perfection proper to it.

The beginning of good in the animal way of life is perfect obedience, progress for it is to gain control of the body and

bring it into subjection, perfection for it is when the habit- \+
ual exercise of virtue has become a pleasure. The beginning
of the rational state is to understand what is set before it
by the teaching of the faith, progress is a life lived in
accordance with that teaching, perfection is when the judgment of the reason passes into a spiritual affection. The
perfection of the rational state is the beginning of the
spiritual state, progress in it is to look upon God's glory
with face uncovered, its perfection is to be transformed into
the same likeness, borrowing glory from that glory, enabled
by the Spirit of the Lord.

The Animal State

To treat in the first place of the first state, animality is a
form of life, which is dominated by the bodily senses, that
is to say, the soul is as it were drawn out of itself by the
bodily senses, engrossed in the pleasure afforded it by the
material things it loves. Thus it finds or nourishes its
sensuality. When it enters into itself again and finds itself
unable to take with it into its spiritual nature the bodies to
which it has become attached by the strong glue of love and
habit, it fashions for itself representations of them and with
these holds friendly converse there.

Since it is accustomed to them and thinks that nothing
exists except what it has left outside or brought back into
itself, it finds its happiness as long as possible in living with
bodily pleasures. When it is separated from them it can
think only by imagining bodies. When it raises itself to
think of spiritual things or the things of God it cannot
conceive of them in any other way than as bodies or bodily
things.

This state turned away from God becomes folly when it is excessively turned back upon itself and so wild that it will not or can not be governed. But when it is torn out of itself by overweening pride it becomes carnal prudence and seems to itself to be wisdom, although it is folly. As the apostle Paul says: "They who claimed to be so wise were made foolish."

However, turned to God this animal state becomes holy simplicity, that is, the will is always the same in its attachment to the same object, as was the case with Job: a simple, upright and God-fearing man. For properly speaking simplicity is a will that is wholly turned toward God, seeking one thing from the Lord with all earnestness, without a desire to disperse its energies in the world. Or again, simplicity is true humility in conversion, more concerned with the inner reality of virtue than with a reputation for it. The simple do not mind seeming to be foolish in the eyes of the world that they may be wise in the sight of God. Or again, simplicity is the will alone fixed on God, not yet formed by reason so as to be love (for that is what a formed will is) nor yet enlightened to be charity, which is the delight of love.

Simplicity then possesses in itself some beginning of God's creation, a simple and good will, the shapeless material, as it were, of what will be a good person. At the outset of conversion it offers this to its Maker to be formed. With good will it has a beginning of wisdom, fear of the Lord. From this it learns that it cannot be formed by itself and that nothing is so advantageous for a fool as to serve a wise master. . . .

On the borders of animality and reason, the kind Creator has placed in the human soul intelligence and inventiveness, and in inventiveness, skill. God established us over the work of his hands and put all this world's things under our feet. To one in the animal state who is proud this comes as a reminder of our natural dignity and of our lost likeness to God, but to one who is simple and humble it serves as a help to recover and keep that likeness.

So it is that what can be known of God is evident within ourselves, that creation gives us some idea of the Creator. So it is that God's justice is known and also the truth that those who do good are worthy of life, while those who act otherwise are worthy of death. . . .

Through countless discoveries of all sorts which we have made, there has come to be in the realms of literature, art and architecture, many branches of learning, many kinds of professions, precisions in scientific research, arts of eloquence, varieties of positions and posts and innumerable investigations into the nature of this world. All avail themselves of these things for their needs and for their advantage, both those who are called wise in this world and those simple ones who are God's sons and daughters. But the former misuse them to satisfy their curiosity, their pleasure and their pride, while the latter make them serviceable as necessity demands, finding their joy elsewhere.

The former, enslaved to their senses and their bodies, reap the fruits of the flesh, which are fornication, uncleanness, impurity, feuds, quarrels, jealousies, outbursts of anger, factions, dissensions, rivalries, debauchery, drunkenness and such like, which make it impossible for those who live in such a way to inherit God's kingdom. Whereas the latter reap the fruits of the spirit, which are charity, joy, peace, patience, kindness, forbearance, generosity, gentleness, faith, temperateness, chastity, continence and the piety which promises well both for this life and for the next.

Both of them engage in action side by side, and to the eyes of all, their deeds are alike, but God sees how different are their wills and intentions. When they return each to him or herself, their conscience shows them the fruits of their intentions. Not, however, that both return to their conscience in the same way, since no one likes to do so after an action who did not go forth from conscience to act with a right intention.

However, those who have not yet mastered their inordinate desires may recollect themselves and find in themselves the effects of those desires: either pleasures which charm them or wounds that are sore. And these give rise to many thoughts. . . . Those who fight against their inordinate desires are harassed by the attachments which they are not yet able completely to overcome. They cannot rid themselves of the imaginations, which spring from their attachments and from the harmful, distracting or idle thoughts to which they are constantly giving birth.

Hence it is that at the time of psalmody or prayer and other spiritual exercises the hearts of God's servants, even though they reject them and struggle against them, are beset with imaginations and fantastic thoughts. Like unclean birds these perch upon them or fly around them so that the sacrifice of their devotion is either snatched from the hand that holds it or, often, defiled to the extent that the offerer is reduced to tears. . . .

The relation of the soul and the body

Since the formation of those in the animal state is wholly or principally concerned with the body and the bearings of the outward person, they must be taught to deaden in accordance with reason those passions in them which belong to earth, and to arbitrate fairly and wisely between the claims of flesh and of spirit, which are constantly at war with each other, showing favor to neither of the two in their judgment.

They must be taught to look upon their bodies as a sick

person, who has been entrusted to their care. They must go against its many wishes in refusing it what is harmful to it and in forcing upon it what is profitable. They must treat it as belonging not to themselves but to him by whom we have been bought at a great price in order that we may glorify him in our bodies.

Again they must be taught to avoid the reproach which the Lord leveled at his sinful people through the prophet Ezekiel: "You have cast me behind your bodies." They must be very careful not to allow their spirit at any time or in any way to fall away from the straight path their vocation sets before them or from the dignity of their nature in order to provide for the needs or the comforts of their bodies.

The body is to be treated strictly, so that it will not rebel or grow wanton. Yet, in such a way that it will be able to serve, for it has been given to the spirit to serve it. It is not to be regarded as the purpose of life but as something without which we cannot live. For we cannot break off the fellowship which we have with the body whenever we want, but we must patiently wait for it to be broken off in the lawful way. In the meantime we must observe the conventions of a valid partnership. We should be on such terms with the body that it would seem we had not long to stay with it, and yet if it should be otherwise we will not be driven out prematurely. . . .

The hold in which, like bilge-water, all temptations and evil and useless thoughts collect is idleness. For the greatest evil which can befall the mind is unemployed leisure. Servants of God should never be idle. But they are to have leisure to devote themselves to God. The name "idleness," which suggests a waste of time and an absence of virility, must not be given to the leisure that is of such unquestionable value, of such holiness, of such seriousness. Is leisure to devote one's time to God idleness? Rather it is the activity of all activities. . . .

In this regard it is ridiculous to take up idle pursuits in order to avoid idleness. A pursuit is idle which either has no usefulness or does not tend to some useful purpose. The aim of activity should not be merely to pass the day more or less enjoyably or at least without becoming too weary of leisure. It should, when the day is over, leave something in the mind that will contribute to the soul's advancement, some new treasure to be added to the heart's store. . . .

Do you ask what you are to do, with what you are to occupy yourself? First of all, after the daily sacrifice of prayer and the time given to *lectio*, every day time should be devoted to the examination of conscience and to the improvement and right ordering of the inner self. . . .

However, serious and prudent persons are ready to undertake all kinds of work and are not distracted by it. Rather, they find it a means to greater recollection. They always keep in sight not so much what they are doing as the purpose of their activity. Thus they aim at the summit of all perfection. The more truly such an effort is made, the more fervently and the more faithfully is manual work done, and all the energies of the body are brought into play. The discipline imposed by good will forces the senses to concentrate. They are left without any opportunity of shaking off the weight of the work to take their pleasure. Brought into humble subjection and service of the spirit, they are taught to adapt themselves to it both in sharing the work and in looking forward to its reward.

Through sin nature has abandoned due order and departed from the uprightness with which it was created. If it turns back to God, it quickly recovers, in proportion to the fear and the love which it has for God, all that it lost by turning away from him. And when the spirit begins to be formed anew to the likeness of the Creator, also the flesh soon takes on fresh life of its own accord and begins to model itself on the reformed spirit. For even contrary to its own inclinations it begins to take delight in whatever delights the spirit. Further, because of its manifold shortcomings, which are the penalty of sin, it thirsts for God in many ways and sometimes even attempts to outstrip its master.

For we do not lose our pleasures, we only transfer them from the body to the soul, from the senses to the spirit. Black bread and plain water, mere greens and vegetables are assuredly no very delectable fare. What does give great pleasure is when, for the love of Christ and the desire of interior delight, a well disciplined stomach is able to satisfy itself with such fare and be thankful. How many thousands of poor people meet the needs of nature with such things or with only one of them? Indeed it would be very easy and enjoyable to live according to nature with the love of God to season it if our folly allowed us. As soon as that is healed, nature finds natural things attractive. It is the same with work. The farm laborer has strong nerves and muscular arms, the result of exercise. But if he is allowed to fall into inactivity, he grows soft. The will leads to action, action induces practice, practice brings strength for all work.

But to return to our subject. In every respect our work and our leisure should never leave us idle. Our occupation should always be that the apostle Paul's words to beginners and those in the animal state may find in us their perfect fulfillment: "I am speaking in human terms, because nature is still strong in you. Just as you once made over your natural powers as slaves to impurity and wickedness till all was wickedness, you must now make over your natural powers as slaves to right-doing till all is sanctified."

Let those in the animal state hear this. Up to the present they have been the willing slaves of their body, but now they are beginning to subject it to the spirit and fit themselves to perceive the things of God. Let them determine to shake off the yoke of so foul a servitude and rid themselves of the bad habits which the flesh has imposed upon them.

Let them set constraint against constraint, habit against habit. Let them cultivate attachments in the place of attachments until they deserve to receive the fullness of a new enjoyment for the old enjoyment. As the apostle Paul recommends, may they at least take as much satisfaction in the absence of worldly and carnal pleasure as they took at first in their presence, and find as great delight in making over their natural powers as slaves to right-doing as they used to find in making them over to the service of impurity and wickedness till all was wickedness. . . .

Spiritual communion

Anyone who has the mind of Christ knows how profitable it is to Christian piety, how fitting and advantageous it is to God's servants, the servants of Christ's redemption, to devote at least one hour of the day to meditating attentively on the benefits conferred by his passion and the redemption he wrought in order to savor them in spirit and store them in the memory. This is spiritually to eat the body of the Lord and drink his blood in remembrance of him who gave to all who believe in him the commandment: Do this in remembrance of me.

Quite apart from the sin of disobedience it is obvious to everyone how impious it would be for us to be mindless of such great loving-kindness on the part of God. It is a crime to forget a friend who at his departure leaves a memorial of himself in whatever form.

Now only a few men, those who have been entrusted with this ministry, are allowed to celebrate in the proper way and place and at the proper time the mystery of this holy and venerable commemoration. But the substance of the mystery can be enacted and handled and received for salvation at all times and in every place where God rules. In the way in which it was given, that is, with due sentiments of devotion, all those can do this to whom are addressed the words: You are a chosen race, a royal priesthood, a consecrated nation, a people God means to have for himself. It is yours to proclaim the exploits of the God who has called you out of darkness into his marvelous light.

The sacrament, while it brings life to one who receives it worthily, can be profaned by an unworthy reception. Then it brings death and judgment. But the substance of the sacrament is only received by the one who is worthy of it and duly prepared. The sacrament without its substance brings death to the communicant. But the substance of the sacrament, even without the visible species, brings eternal life.

Now if you wish and if you truly desire it, this is at your disposal at all hours of day and night. As often as you stir up sentiments of piety and faith in calling to mind what he did when he suffered for you, you eat his body and drink his blood. As long as you remain in him through love and he in you through the sanctity and justice, he works in you. You are reckoned as belonging to his body and counted as one of his members.

Lectio divina

At fixed hours time should be given to certain definite reading. For haphazard reading, constantly varied and as if lighted upon by chance, does not edify but makes the mind unstable. Taken into the memory lightly, it goes out from it even more lightly. But you should concentrate on certain authors and let your mind grow accustomed to them.

The scriptures need to be read and understood in the same spirit in which they were written. You will never enter into Paul's meaning until by constant application to reading him and by giving yourself to constant meditation you have imbibed his spirit. You will never understand David until by experience you have made the sentiments of the psalms your own. And that applies to all scripture. There is the same gulf between attentive *lectio* and mere reading as there is between friendship and acquaintance with a passing guest, between boon companionship and chance meeting.

Each day, some part of your daily reading should also be committed to memory, taken as it were into the stomach, to be more carefully digested and brought up again for frequent rumination. Something in keeping with your vocation and helpful to concentration, something that will take hold of the mind and save it from distraction.

Reading should also stimulate the feelings and give rise to prayer, which should interrupt your reading, an interruption which should not so much hamper the reading as restore to it a mind ever more purified for understanding.

For reading serves the purpose of the intention with which it is done. If the reader truly seeks God in reading, everything that is read tends to promote that end, making the mind surrender in the course of the reading and bring all that is understood into Christ's service. But if the intention of the reader is directed elsewhere it draws everything in its wake. Nothing that it finds in scripture is too holy or too religious not to be applied to its own perverseness or folly through the pursuit of vainglory or a distortion of meaning or a wrong understanding. For all the scriptures demand that readers should approach them in the fear of the Lord. In that fear, first of all they should make their intention steadfast. Then from it should derive all their understanding and appreciation of what they read and the proper ordering of it.

Spiritual exercises should never be laid aside in favor of bodily ones for any length of time nor totally, but the mind should learn to return to them easily and give itself to bodily exercises while still being attached to the things of the spirit. As has already been said, it is not the spiritual things that are for the sake of the bodily but the bodily that are for the sake of the spiritual. By bodily exercises in the present context we mean those which involve manual work.

There are also other exercises at which the body must toil, such as vigils, fasts and the like. They are no hindrance to spiritual things but help them if they are done with reason and discretion. However, through the vice of indiscretion they can be practiced in such a way that the spirit grows faint or the body is enfeebled. Then spiritual growth is hampered. Those who so behave cheat their body of the effects of good work, their spirit of its affections, their neighbor of good example and God of honor. They are guilty of sacrilege and responsible to God for all this damage.

As the apostle Paul teaches, however, it is not contrary to human nature or unfitting or undue or unjust to have an occasional headache in God's service. The pursuit of worldly vanity has previously brought many a headache. The same is true of hunger even when the stomach audibly protests. It was often stuffed to the point of vomiting. But in all things due measure should be observed. The body should be mortified at times but not broken. For even bodily training is of some value, not very great but nonetheless useful.

Therefore some care should be taken of the flesh, but not to the extent that would foster inordinate desires. This care should be moderate and involve a certain amount of spiritual discipline so that in manner, quality and quantity it befits God's servant.

For what seems base in us we should surround with special honor, while what is seemly in us has no such need. We should present the whole of our life, however hidden it may be from others, as holy and honorable before God. All our behavior should be such that the angels may look upon it with pleasure, even though it all takes place within the walls of our dwelling. . . .

So whether you eat or drink or what ever else you do, do all in the name of the Lord, devoutly, reverently and religiously.

If you eat, let sobriety adorn a table which is already spare. When you eat, do not give yourself wholly to the business of eating. While the body is securing its refreshment, let not the mind wholly neglect its own nourishment. Let it dwell upon and as it were digest something that it recalls of the Lord's sweetness, a passage from the scriptures that will feed it as it meditates upon it. The bodily need itself should be satisfied not in a worldly or carnal way but as befits a servant of God. Even from the point of view of health, the more becoming and orderly the manner of eating, the easier and more wholesome is the process of digestion.

Watch must be kept on the manner and the time of eating, on the quality and quantity of the food. All superfluity and seasonings that only adulterate food should be shunned.

Watch must be kept on the manner, so that eaters do not pour their souls over everything they eat. Watch on the time, lest the hour be anticipated, and the quality. . . .

Pardon, Lord, pardon. We invent excuses and find pretexts, but there is no one who can hide from the light of your truth, which not only enlightens the converted but also strikes those who turn away. Not even the bones you made to be hidden within us are hidden from you. And yet we make them hidden to ourselves, for there is scarcely any who in these things which concern you is willing to make trial of what they can do. But that they find it possible to do, without the least hesitation, whenever it is a question of worldly or carnal gains and they are driven by fear or drawn by cupidity. But even if we deceive others who do not know us, do not allow us, as if attempting to deceive you, to deceive ourselves. . . .

Prayer

Beginners in the animal state, Christ's raw recruits, should be taught to draw near to God so that God in turn may draw near to them. For such is the prophet's exhortation: Draw near to God, and he will draw near to you. We have not only to be created and formed but also endowed with life. For first God formed the human person, then he breathed into that person's face the breath of life so that the person became a living soul. The formation of a person is our moral training, our life is the love of God.

This is conceived by faith, brought forth by hope, formed and endowed with life by charity, that is, by the Holy Spirit infusing himself into our love and spirit, attracting us to himself. Then God loves himself in us and makes us his spirit and his love, one with himself. For as the body has no means of living apart from its spirit, so our affections, which are called love, have no means of living, that is to say of loving God, but the Holy Spirit.

Now the love of God in us, which is born of grace, is fed with the milk of reading, nourished with the food of meditation, strengthened and enlightened by prayer. The best and safest reading matter and subject for meditation for those in the animal state, newly come to Christ, to train them in the interior life, is the outward actions of our Redeemer. In them they should find an example of humility, a stimulus to charity and to sentiments of piety. Likewise from the sacred scriptures and the writings of the holy Fathers it is those parts which deal with morality and are easier to understand that should be put before them.

They should also be given the lives of the saints and the accounts of their martyrdoms. They should not trouble themselves with historical details but should always find something to stir their beginner's mind to love God and turn from themselves. The reading of other narratives gives pleasure but does not edify. Rather they distract the mind and at the time of prayer and meditation cause all manner of useless or harmful thoughts to surge up from the memory. The nature of the reading determines the quality of the subsequent meditation. The reading of difficult works tires the unpracticed mind instead of refreshing it. It shatters its powers of concentration and dulls its understanding.

Beginners should be taught to raise their hearts on high in their prayer, to pray spiritually. They should keep as far away as they can from material objects or their representations when they think of God. They should be exhorted to direct their attention with all the purity of heart they can muster to him to whom they are offering the sacrifice of prayer. They are to advert to themselves the offerers and to appreciate what they are offering and what is its quality. For to the extent that they see or understand him to whom they are making their offering, they reach out to him with their affections. Love itself is understanding for them. And to the extent that this love animates their affections they realize that their offering is worthy of God. And so all is well with them.

Yet it is better and safer, as has already been said, to put before such beginners when they are praying or meditating, a representation of our Lord's humanity — of his birth, passion and resurrection—so that the weak spirit, which is only able to think of material objects, may have something to which it can apply itself and cling with devout attention as befits its degree. Christ presents himself in his character of mediator. As we read in Job: "Those who contemplate their own form do not sin." When beginners concentrate their powers upon Christ, thinking of God in human form, they do not wholly depart from the truth. As long as their faith does not separate God from the human, they will learn eventually to grasp God in the human.

In this matter, those who are poorer in spirit and more simple children of God find as a rule that at first their feelings are the sweeter the nearer they are to human nature. Afterwards, however, faith becomes a movement of love, and in the midst of their hearts with love's sweet embrace they embrace Christ Jesus, wholly man because of the human nature he took to himself, wholly God because it was God who took the nature. Then they begin to know him no longer according to the flesh, although they are not yet fully able to conceive of him in his divinity. And enthroning him in their hearts they love to offer him the vows which their lips have uttered: supplications, prayers, entreaties, in keeping with the time and the matter.

Some prayers are short and simple as they are formed by the will. Or they meet a need of the moment of the one who is praying. Others are longer and more intellectual as in search of the truth; asking, seeking, knocking until they receive, find and the door is opened to them. Others are winged, proceeding from the spirit and bearing rich fruit, expressing the affections which accompany fruition and the joy of illuminating grace. The apostle Paul enumerates these kinds of prayer in a different order: supplications, prayers, petitions and thanksgiving

Petition is what we put in the first place. It is concerned with obtaining temporal benefits and what is necessary for this life. When we make petitions, God indeed approves our good will, but he follows his own better judgment and enables us who make petition in the right spirit to acquiesce in his will. It is of this that the psalmist says: My prayer is still for what pleases them, that is to say, what pleases even the godless. All alike but especially the children of this world desire the tranquillity of peace, bodily health, good weather and whatever else contributes to a right use of this life and the satisfying of its needs, even what serves the pleasure of those who make ill use of life. Those who in faith make their petitions for these intentions, although they only ask for them to meet their needs, nonetheless they always submit their will to the will of God.

Supplication is a troubled and insistent turning to God during one's spiritual exercises. . . .

Prayer is the affection of those who cling to God, a certain familiar and devout conversation, a state in which the enlightened mind enjoys God as long as it is permitted.

Thanksgiving is an unwearying and undistracted attention of the good will to God in understanding and acknowledging God's grace. Sometimes outward activity or interior affection is not there or sluggish as the apostle Paul says: Praiseworthy intentions are always ready at hand, but I cannot find my way to the performance of them. As if to say: Good will indeed is always present, but a times it is ineffective because although I seek to perform some good work I do not find the means. This is charity which never fails.

It is of uninterrupted prayer or thanksgiving of which the apostle Paul says: "Pray without interruption and give thanks at all times." For it is a certain unchanging goodness of the mind and of the well-ordered spirit and a certain resemblance to the goodness of their Father God, on the part of God's children. It prays for everyone always and gives thanks for everything. It continually pours itself out before God in as many kinds of prayer or thanksgiving as its devout affection finds occasion in its needs or consolations and also in sharing its neighbor's pain or joys. It is constantly absorbed in thanksgiving, because to be in such a state is to be always in the joy of the Holy Spirit.

When it is a question of petitions, prayer should be made

devoutly and with faith but without obstinate persistence, since it is not we but our Father who is in heaven who knows what we need in these temporal things.

But when it is a question of supplications, then we should persist, yet with all humility and patience, because it is only in patience that they bear fruit. Sometimes when grace is not quick in coming to the assistance, the supplicants find the heavens become bronze and the ground iron. When the hardness of their hearts left to itself does not deserve to have its prayers heard, those in need think in their anxiety that they are being refused what in fact is only being withheld for a time. And when like the Canaanite woman they lament that they are being ignored and scorned, they imagine that their past sins are being imputed to them or made a matter of reproach like the uncleanness of a dog.

Sometimes, however, by dint of hard work, they obtain when they ask, they find when they seek, the door is opened to them when they knock. The toil of supplication is found worthy to obtain at length the consolations and sweetnesses of prayer.

Sometimes also the affections of pure prayer and sweetness do not have to be looked for but take the initiative. Without being asked for or sought, without any knocking, grace takes us by surprise. It is as if one belonging to the servant class was welcomed to the table at which the children of the family eat. A soul that is still untrained and a beginner is taken up into the state of prayer which, as a rule, is given to the perfect after they have earned it as a reward for their sanctity. When this happens it comes as a judgment, making it impossible for the negligent soul to be unaware of what it is neglecting, or as a stimulus to charity, kindling love in the soul for the grace that offers itself so freely.

In this matter, alas, very many are deceived. Fed as they are with the bread of the children, they consider that they are in fact children now. They begin to fall back from the point from which they should be advancing. The result of the grace which came to them is that they play their conscience false, considering themselves to be of some importance, whereas in fact they are nothing. The Lord's gifts do not lead to any improvement in them but to a hardening of heart so that they join those of whom the psalm says: "The Lord's enemies have lied to him, and they will last to the end of the ages. Yet he fed them with rich grain and filled them with honey from the rock." Servants as they are, they are fed by God the Father with the more choice food of grace so that they may aspire to be children. But they turn God's grace to ill account and become his enemies. . . .

The Rational State

To pass on then from the animal state to the rational, so that from the rational we may pass on to the spiritual (and would that this transition in our treatment of the subject might be accompanied by a corresponding advance in reality), we must first of all know that Wisdom, as we read in the book that bears its name, "anticipates those who desire it and comes to meet them, joyfully revealing itself to them on the way." Whether it be in the effort to advance either in meditation or in study, "it reaches everywhere on account of its purity." For God helps with his countenance those who look upon him. The splendor of the Highest Good moves and leads onward and attracts those who contemplate it. . . .

Now there is no more worthy or more useful exercise for us who are endowed with reason than that which involves our best endowment, our mind or soul. By this we are made superior to the other animals, and it is superior to the other parts of ourselves. For the mind or soul, there is nothing more worthy to seek or sweeter to find or more useful to possess than the one thing which is superior to the mind: God himself.

He is not far from any of us, for it is in him that we live and move and have our being. But not in the same way as with the air. In him we live through faith, we move and advance through hope, we have our being, that is our fixed dwelling place, through love.

It was by him and for him that the rational soul was created, that its yearning might be for him and that he should be its good. It is from his goodness that it is good. It was created to his image and likeness in order that as long as its life here lasts it may approach as nearly and as truly as possible to him by likeness from whom only unlikeness brings about distance. In this way the soul will be holy here as God is holy, and in the next life happy as he is happy.

In a word all greatness and goodness for the soul that is great and good consists in looking upon and wondering at and aspiring to what is above it, so that the devoted image hastens to cling to its exemplar. The soul is the image of God. This fact enables it to understand that it can and should cling to him.

On earth the soul rules the body, which has been entrusted to it by its better part, memory, understanding and love. But it prefers always to be engaged in the place from whence it knows that it has received all that it is, all that it has. There it hopes, to the extent we can hope if we do not fail to bring our life into line with our holy hope, to dwell forever and, with the full vision of God, to attain to a full likeness to him.

There it is that the soul's gaze is fixed. From there it depends. It lives with others more to impart to them God's life. It seeks to obtain the things of God more than to animate this mortal and human life.

The soul holds the body which it animates erect, raising it to its natural state of looking towards heaven, which by nature, place and dignity transcends all places and all bodies. Because of its spiritual nature, it loves to look to the things which are higher in the spiritual order, to God and the things of God, not by savoring proud thoughts but by loving devoutly and living soberly and justly and piously. The higher the goal to which it aspires, the more vigorous must be the pursuits in which it exercises itself. They must not only tint it but dye it thoroughly. Their effect on it must be to bring it to perfection. . . .

With regard to vices, we are more afraid of the evil desires which arise within ourselves than of assaults coming from other people. We fear infection more than violence. By dint of much hard work and persevering effort, the virtues come to influence our affections and give us the right outlook. On the other hand the vices avail themselves of the slightest relaxation or disorder to insinuate themselves into our character and become as it were natural.

But no vice is natural to us, whereas virtue is. Nonetheless the force of habits, which come from a corrupt will or prolonged carelessness, tend to make a host of vices become, as it were, natural to the conscience which has been neglected. As the philosopher says, habit is second nature.

Yet every bad spirit can be softened before it grows hard in evil. And even after it has become hardened it need not be despaired of. For the cure pronounced upon Adam means that the earth and the ground which we cultivate, which are our heart and body, while they produce harmful or useless growth freely in all directions, can with hard work produce what is useful and necessary.

However, since virtue is natural to us, when eventually it comes into the soul, it comes not indeed without hard work, yet as to its own proper place. And there it settles down to stay. Nature is well pleased with it, for the soul knows no greater reward than to be aware of itself in God.

Vice, however, although it is considered to be nothing other than the privation of virtue, can assume such enormous proportions as to be felt crushing and overwhelming. Its vileness can be such that it defiles and infects. It can cling with so pertinacious a force of habit that nature is scarcely able to shake it off.

It is in vain that every rivulet of vice is dried up if the source is not stopped up. For example, a will that has slackened leads to levity of mind, from which there proceed instability of disposition, inconstancy in behavior, empty-headed joy that often reaches the point of carnal indulgence, and groundless sorrow that sometimes causes even bodily sickness. And other evils may arise from the vice of levity and lead to neglect or abandonment of vocation. So also a will that has grown proud through habit often inflates the soul with pride while the heart is dried up. From such a state of affairs there proceed vainglory, trust of oneself, neglect of God, boasting, disobedience, scorn, presumption and the other diseases of the spirit, which usually arise from conceit and the habit of pride.

In this way every kind of vice derives its origin from some disorder of the will or from the force of bad habit. The longer a vice has grown in the mind, the more tenaciously it clings and the stronger are the remedies it calls for. The more painstaking the care it needs. . . .

But let us return to the praise of virtue. What is virtue? It is the daughter of reason but still more of grace. It is a certain force issuing from nature, but it derives from grace the fact that it is virtue. The approving judgment of reason makes it a force, but the desire of an enlightened will makes it virtue. For virtue is a willing assent to good. Virtue is a certain balance of life, conforming to reason in all things.

Virtue is the use of free will according to the judgment of reason. Virtue is a certain humility, a certain patience. It embraces obedience, prudence, temperance, fortitude, justice and very many other qualities in each of which virtue is nothing other than, as has been said, the use of free will in accordance with the judgment of reason.

For a will that is good is the source of all good in the soul and the mother of all virtues. Contrariwise an evil will gives rise to all evil and vices. Therefore, those who keep guard over their souls should be very anxious in their watch over their wills, so that they may understand and discern wisely what is or ought to be the total object of volition, the love of God, and what is willed because of it, for example, love of neighbor. . . .

In the love of God all reason and all discretion amount to this: As he in his love for us went to the limit of love so, if possible, we should love him without any limit. Happy the one whose desire to keep the Lord's commandments is without bounds.

Although the gift of self which is prompted by love should be without any limit or bounds, external activity should be kept within fixed limits and governed by rule. In this regard, to prevent excesses on the part of the will, truth must always be present, keeping guard by means of obedience.

For nothing is of greater advantage to one who is making progress on the way to God than will and truth. These are the two of whom our Lord says: "If they agree in asking for anything, whatever it may be, they will obtain it from God, their Father."

If these two things are in perfect accord, combining to form one principle, they contain in themselves all the plenitude of the virtues without the interference of any vice. They are capable of anything even in those who have no strength. They are endowed with everything and possess everything in those who have no possessions. They give, lend, contribute, make themselves useful in those who are living quietly in retirement. There are glory and wealth in the conscience of those holy ones, issuing from the fruits of their good will. Externally they are protected not only on one side, as with the shields of this world, but on all sides by the shield of God's truth. For interiorly they are made always cheerful and pleasant by good will while in outward activity truth keeps them grave and serious, safe and assured. Therefore these men and women rise above the things of this world and are always tranquil as we hear of the air above the moon.

The will

The will is a natural appetite of the soul with various objects: now God and the interior life, now the body and external things relating to the body.

When the will mounts on high like fire going up to its proper place, that is to say, when it unites with truth and tends to higher things, it is "love." When it is fed with the milk of grace in order to make progress it is "dilection." When it lays hold of its object and keeps it in its grasp and has enjoyment of it, it is "charity," it is unity of spirit, it is God. For God is charity. But in these matters we are only beginning when we arrive at the end, for they do not admit of full perfection in this life.

When the will turns aside to the things of the flesh, it is carnal concupiscence. When it is governed by worldly curiosity, it is concupiscence of the eyes. When it makes glory or honor its ambition, it is the pride of life.

Yet as long as in such things it serves the advantages or necessities of nature, it is nature or natural appetite. When, however, it abandons itself to superfluous or harmful objects, it is a vice of nature or a vicious will. You will find the proof of this in yourself, in the first movement of desire.

When it is a question of bodily necessities, and the will goes no further than the first desire, it is the soul's natural appetite. But when its desires extend ever further and further, it betrays itself. It is no longer will but a vice of the will, avarice or covetousness or something of that sort. For the will is soon satisfied in such matters, while its vices never have enough.

In spiritual things and matters relating to God, the will is praiseworthy when it takes as its object something that is within truth. When it wills something outside or exceeding its possibilities, it must be governed and checked. When it does not will what is within its reach, it must be aroused and stimulated. For often if it is not kept in check it breaks away and rushes headlong to disaster. Often if it is not stirred up it sleeps and delays, forgets its destination and easily turns aside, letting itself be caught in the shackles of any pleasure that may offer itself. . . . Someone else, someone whose will is not a prey to the same fervor, is often a better judge of our acts than we are. For, either through negligence or through self-love, we often have a mistaken idea of ourselves.

Therefore obedience is a trusty guardian of the will, whether it be obedience to a command or to advice, whether it involve subordinates or be prompted by charity alone. For, as the apostle Paul says, those who practice obedience often cleanse their hearts more effectively and more smoothly by submitting to their equals or even to their inferiors in the obedience of charity than by the subjection to their superiors in the obedience of necessity. In the former case it is charity alone that orders or advises and obeys, while in the latter there is the fear of punishment or the threat of an imperious authority or constraining necessity. In the former case greater glory is owing to the one who obeys, while in the latter disobedience incurs greater punishment.

It is clear to all, therefore, how necessary it is for those whose hearts are raised on high that their wills should have due custody to govern, regulate and order the exterior, but even more for the sake of the interior. For when a soul often thinks of itself or of God, the will is the starting point of all its thoughts, and it is by this starting point that the whole character of its thinking is determined.

The Spiritual State

When the object of thought is God and the things of God, and the will reaches the stage at which it becomes love, the Holy Spirit, the spirit of life, at once infuses himself by way of love. He gives life to everything, lending his assistance in prayer, in meditation or in the study of human weakness. Immediately the memory becomes wisdom and tastes with relish the good things of the Lord, while the thoughts to which they give rise are brought to the intellect to be formed into affection. The understanding of the one thinking becomes the contemplation of one loving, and it shapes it into certain experiences of spiritual and divine sweetness, which it brings before the spirit so that the spirit rejoices in them.

And then, insofar as it is possible for us, worthy thoughts are entertained of God, if indeed the word "thought" is correct. There is no impelling principle nor anything impelled but only awareness of God's abundant sweetness leading to exultation, jubilation and a true experience of the Lord in goodness on the part of those who have sought him in this simplicity of heart.

But this way of thinking about God does not lie at the disposal of the thinker. It is a gift of grace, bestowed by the

Holy Spirit who breathes where he chooses, how he chooses and upon whom he chooses. Our part is continually to prepare our heart by ridding our will of foreign attachments, our reason or intellect of anxieties, our memory of ideas or absorbing thoughts, even sometimes of necessary business, so that in the Lord's good time and when he sees fit, at the sound of the Holy Spirit's breathing, the elements which constitute thought may be immediately free to come together and do their work. Each contributes its share to the joy of the soul: the will, pure affection for the joy which the Lord gives; the memory, faithful material; the intellect, the sweetness of experience.

A will that is neglected gives rise to thoughts that are idle and unworthy of God. A will that is corrupted produces thoughts that are perverse and alienated from God. A rightly ordered will leads to thoughts that are necessary for the living of this life. A dutiful will engenders thoughts which are rich in the fruits of the Spirit and bring the enjoyment of God. "Now the fruits of the Spirit," the apostle Paul tells us, "are charity, joy, peace, patience, forbearance, goodness, kindness, meekness, faith, modesty, chastity, continence."

In every kind of thought, all that occurs in the mind conforms to the intention of the will through the intervention of God's mercy and judgment. The just person is made still more just and the one who is defiled becomes still more defiled.

Those who desire to love the Lord or already love him should always question their spirit and examine their conscience as to what is their overall desire and what they desire for the sake of this. They should also ask what else the spirit wills or hates and what inordinate desires the flesh entertains in opposition to it.

Desires which make their way in as if from outside and then disappear are not something we will but only idle thoughts. The same is true of those thoughts which brush against the soul in passing, so that at one moment it feels desire and at the next moment feels none. They may even go as far as to cause the mind some pleasure, but the mind quickly shakes itself free of them if it is its own master.

As to the basic desire, first of all the object of desire should be considered, then the extent to which it is desired and the way in which it is desired. If our basic desire is for God, we should examine how much and in what way we desire God. Do we love him to the point of turning away from ourselves and everything which exists or can exist? And do we do this not only in accord with the reason but also following the mind's inclination? Then the will is now something more than will; it is love, dilection, charity and unity of spirit.

For such is the way in which God is to be loved. "Love" is a strong inclination of the will toward God. "Dilection" is a clinging to him or a union with him. "Charity" is the enjoyment of him. But those whose hearts are set on high, "unity of spirit" with God is the term of the will's progress toward God. No longer does it merely desire what God desires, not only does it love him, but its love is perfect so that it can will only what God wills.

Now to will what God wills is already to be like God. To be able to will only what God wills is already to be what God is. For him to will and to be are the same thing. Therefore it is well said that we shall see him fully as he is when we are like him, that is, when we are what he is. For those who have been enabled to become sons or daughters of God have been enabled to become not indeed God, but what God is: holy and in the future fully happy as God is. And the source of their present holiness and their future happiness is none other than God himself, who is at once their holiness and their happiness.

Perfection

Resemblance to God is the whole of our perfection. To refuse to be perfect is to be at fault. Therefore the will must always be trained for perfection and love made ready. The will must be prevented from dissipating itself on foreign objects, love preserved from defilement. For this alone were we created, for we live to be like God. We were created in his image.

There is a likeness of God that is lost only with life itself. It is left with us by the Creator as evidence of a better and more sublime likeness that has been lost. It is possessed regardless of acceptance or refusal, alike by those who are capable of understanding it and by those who are so stupid that they cannot conceive it. It consists in this: Just as God is everywhere and is wholly present in every part of his creation, so the soul is present in the body. God is never unlike himself and without any unlikeness carries our dissimilar operations in his creation. So also our soul vivifies the whole of the body with one and the same life, in the bodily senses and in the thoughts of the heart, and without any unlikeness it is constantly carrying out dissimilar operations. As far as merit is concerned this likeness to God in us is of no importance with God, since it derives from nature, not from will or effort.

But there is another likeness, one closer to God, inasmuch as it is freely willed. It consists in the virtues and inspires the soul as it were to imitate the greatness of the Supreme Good by the greatness of its virtue, and his unchangeable eternity by its unwearying perseverance in good.

In addition there is yet another likeness of which something has been already said. It is so close in its resemblance that it is styled not merely a likeness but unity of spirit. It makes us one with God, one spirit, not only with the unity which comes of willing the same thing but with a greater fullness of virtue, as has been said: the inability to will anything else.

It is called unity of spirit not only because the Holy Spirit brings it about or inclines our spirit to it. It is the Holy Spirit himself, the God who is charity. He is the love of Father and Son, their unity, sweetness, good, kiss, embrace and whatever else they can have in common in that supreme unity of truth and truth of unity. In the manner appropriate for us, the Holy Spirit becomes for us in regard to God what he is for the Son in regard to the Father and for the Father in regard to the Son through a unity of substance. The soul in its happiness finds itself in the midst of the embrace and kiss of Father and Son. In a manner which exceeds description and thought, we are found worthy to become not God but what God is, that is to say, we become through grace what God is by nature.

That is why in his list of spiritual exercises the apostle Paul knowingly inserted the Holy Spirit. He says: "In chastity, in knowledge, in forbearance, in graciousness, in the Holy Spirit, in unfeigned charity, in the word of truth, in the power of God." See how he put the Holy Spirit in the midst of the good virtues, like the heart in the middle of the body, doing and ordering everything, imparting life to everything.

For he is the almighty Artificer, who creates our good will in regard to God, inclines God to be merciful to us, shapes our desire, gives strength, ensures the prosperity of undertakings, conducts all things powerfully, and disposes everything sweetly.

The Holy Spirit it is who gives life to our spirit and holds it together, just as it gives life to its body and holds it together. We may teach how to seek God, and angels may teach how to adore him, but the Holy Spirit alone teaches how to find him, possess him and enjoy him. The Holy

Spirit himself is the anxious quest of those who truly seek, he is the devotion of those who adore in spirit and truth. He is the wisdom of those who find, the love of those who possess, the gladness of those who enjoy.

Yet, whatever he bestows here on his faithful of the vision and the knowledge of God, it is in a mirror and a riddle, as far removed from the vision and the knowledge that is to be in the future as faith is from truth or time from eternity.

The Icon

William sensed his end was near and his life's work done. In this frame of mind he consoled himself and gratified others by undertaking the writing of a biography of his beloved friend, Bernard of Clairvaux. Bernard had profoundly influenced his life and had given it its deepest meaning. In those days a biography was an essential element for bringing about the recognition of a person as a saint. This is what William and Bernard's other friends had in view. For this purpose William had to follow the accepted pattern and write a story full of miracles and wondrous happenings, medieval hagiography, Christian mythology at its richest. Given all that, Bernard still remained for William the exemplar of Christian life at its deepest, fullest and most realized.

But William was not a blind admirer. Himself a man of great moderation, who had clearly taught moderation in his own writings and life, William could not be wholly in sympathy with Bernard's excesses. He tries to respect them and notes that the saint himself later accused himself of excess and was accused by zealous novices of preaching excessive moderation. In this way William, even as he offers Bernard as an icon of Christian life, yet calls for prudent moderation in one's practices—not in one's total love.

We offer here but a few brief passages from William's *Life of Bernard*, those in particular where William shares his own intimate experience of the saint and of the saint's community. They tell us as much about William and his ideals as they do about Bernard of Clairvaux.

159

The First Life of Saint Bernard

Preface

If you will grant me your favor and aid, O Lord, it is my aim to write the life of your servant and thereby give honor and praise to your name. It was he whom you did use to make the Church of our day shine with grace and holiness, such as was common in the days of the apostles but has seldom been seen since. I call upon your love to help me in this work, for it is love of you that inspires me to write it. It does not really matter how little we may feel the warmth of your love permeating our hearts, for when we see such an outstanding witness to your honor and glory casting its light upon the world, we must do all we can to ensure that this light which you have kindled is hidden from none of your children. When you can make its brightness seen more clearly through your works, my pen in comparison seems but a poor means of showing this light and raising it on high before men and women. Even so, through my humble effort, may its brightness shine on all who dwell in your house.

I, for one, have long wanted to perform this task, but either fear or timidity has always held me back. Sometimes I would be obsessed with the idea that the subject was too wonderful or holy for me to attempt and that it should be left to someone worthier than myself. Other moments found me thinking that it would be better to write his life after his death—if, that is, I were to outlive him—for then he would not be too embarrassed when praises were heaped upon him, and the work would not give rise to so much unpleasant argument and disagreement. But the fact is that he is still alive and thriving — indeed, it almost seems as though he grows stronger with weaker health — and he is still performing deeds which are well worth recording and which seem to be each more wonderful than the last. Such things cry out for someone to note them down, for he is not likely to speak about them himself.

Even now the sands of my life are running out, and my body, in the grip of illness and weakness, will soon be answering the call of death. I am certain that the time is not far off when I must leave this life and appear before my Creator. I fear that I may already be too late to start and finish a book that I dearly want to complete before my life ebbs out. . . .

I have undertaken to record this life, because I wished to ensure that the facts should not be spread about in a way that was only partially true, but that they should instead be brought together and linked up so as to form one continuous history. I must make it clear that I do not want this book published while Bernard is still alive, for it has been written without his knowledge or consent. But I pray God that after his death and after my span of years is finished, someone may come forward to complete what I have tried to do to the best of my ability, for anyone else will, I know, be more competent and more worthy to write about so holy a subject. Those who take this work upon themselves after me will be able to write not only about the wonderful deeds that Bernard performed, and which can be seen by anyone who cares to look, but also about the outstanding holiness of his soul, which God alone can know fully. They will be able to show that his death was just as precious as his life in the Lord's sight, proving the holiness of his life from the holiness of his death and the holiness of his death from the holiness of his life.

William's first visit to Bernard

When I first went to see him with another abbot, I found him in that little hut of his, which was just like the kind of shack built for lepers at cross-roads. I found him completely free from all the spiritual and temporal problems involved in the ruling of any monastery. This was exactly what the bishop had commanded. As a result Bernard was able to open the innermost depths of his soul to the action of God's loving grace and to enjoy in his silence and solitude delights such as are the reward of the blessed in heaven.

Going into the hovel, which had become a palace by his presence in it, and thinking what a wonderful person dwelt in such a despicable place, I was filled with such awe of the hut itself that I felt as if I were approaching the very altar of God. And the sweetness of his character so attracted me to him and filled me with such desire to share his life amid such poverty and simplicity, that if the chance had then been given to me I should have asked nothing more than to be allowed to remain with him always, looking after him and ministering to his needs. Bernard himself received us cheerfully. When we asked after his health he replied with that charming smile of his: "I am very well in spite of the fact that, although reasonable men used to give me their obedience, God's wisdom has now put me under obedience to an irrational brute." This remark was a reference to a certain proud and boorish man, who had boasted that he could cure Bernard of his illness, although in fact he really knew nothing about medicine. Nevertheless, Bernard had been told by Bishop William, together with the abbots of the general chapter and his brethren at Clairvaux, to follow all this man's instructions. . . .

Although unworthy of so great a privilege, I remained with him for a few days, and as I looked about me I thought that I was gazing on a new heaven and a new earth, for it seemed as though there were tracks freshly made by men of our own day in the path that had first been trodden by our fathers, the Egyptian monks of long ago.

The golden age of Clairvaux

This was indeed the golden age of Clairvaux. Virtuous men, who had once held honors and riches in the world, lovingly embraced a life of poverty in Christ. And thus they helped to plant the Church of God by giving their lives in toil and hardship, in hunger and thirst, in cold and exposure, in insult and persecutions and many difficulties, just like the apostle Paul. These were the men who made it possible for Clairvaux to enjoy the peace and sufficiency which it has today, for they did not regard their lives as being lived only on their own account but for Christ's sake and for the benefit of the brethren who would serve God in the monastery in years to come. They did not think selfishly of their own poverty and lack of even the necessities of life. It is through the hardships and efforts faced by them that there is now enough to supply the monastery with all that is needed, without dulling the realization that a monk's life is one of voluntary poverty for Christ's sake.

People who come down from the hills into the valley of Clairvaux for the first time are struck by an awareness that God dwells there, for the simplicity and unpretentiousness of the buildings in the quiet valley betrays the lowly and simple life led by the monks for the sake of Christ. They find that the silence of the deep of night reigns even in the middle of the day, although in this valley full of men there are no idle souls. Everyone busies himself with the tasks entrusted to him. The only sound that can be heard is the sound of the brethren at work or singing their office in praise of God. Even usually worldly men are filled with much awe by this atmosphere of silence, with the result that not only are they slow to indulge in any idle or improper chatter but keep their talking to a minimum.

The loneliness of this place, hidden among the woods and closed in by the surrounding hills, was comparable to the cave where the shepherds found our holy father Saint Benedict, so closely did the monks of Clairvaux follow his form of life and style of dwelling. Although they all lived together, it may be said that they were all solitaries, for although the valley was full of men the harmony and charity that reigned there were such that each monk seemed to be there all by himself. We all know well that the unstable are alone even when they are by themselves, and in the same way among those whose lives are under the stabilizing influence of the rule in silence and unity of purpose, the way of life itself helps to establish an inner solitude in the depths of the heart.

The monks' diet matched the simplicity of their dwellings. The bread was produced by the toil of the brethren from the almost barren earth of the desert place, and it seemed to be made more of grit than of grain. As with all their other food they ate, it had almost no flavor but that which hunger and gratitude to God lent it. But the simplicity of the fervent novices used to overstep its mark when they refused God's own gifts lest they destroy the grace within them. For they thought that anything that was a pleasure to eat was a poison to their souls. The zeal of their father in Christ had so trained them in what their physique could bear that they did constantly and without complaint —nay, even with actual pleasure—things that would at first sight seem impossible for any living person. But the pleasure that they took in such mortification gave rise to another kind of murmuring and complaint, which was all the more dangerous, because it seemed to them that their complaint was concerned more with matters of the spirit than the welfare of the body. They were quite resolved and convinced by their own experience that any pleasure taken by the body would be harmful to the soul and that they had to carefully avoid anything that the body found enjoyable. For they thought, like the wise men in the gospel, that they could return to their own country of heaven by another way, since the sweetness of the love within their souls allowed them to find equal delight in pleasant and unpleasant things. And thus they thought that their lives as monks in such a secluded spot were much more pleasurable than the lives they had formerly lived in the world.

On this matter they began to be a little suspicious of the daily sermons in chapter addressed to them by their abbot, for he seemed to give more consideration to the body than to the soul. At length they asked the opinion of Bishop William of Chalons, who was at Clairvaux at the time. That eloquent and holy man spoke to them on the subject worrying them. He ended his words on this note: that anyone who refused God's gifts in order to safeguard the grace within his soul was in fact rebelling against God's grace and resisting the Holy Spirit. He reminded them of the incident in the life of the prophet Eliseo and of the sons of the prophets, who lived with him as hermits in the desert. At the hour for their meal they discovered a certain deadly bitterness in their broth. Then the prophet turned the bitterness into sweetness by pouring a little flour into the cooking pot. The holy bishop concluded with these words: "The broth in this story is the same as your broth, for both are bitter and repulsive. But the flour which turns that bitterness into sweetness is the grace of God working within you. You may, then, eat it without danger and thank God for the change he has wrought. By his grace he has made fit for your use and consumption what in its natural state was not fit for humans. If you continue in your disobedience and disbelief you will be resisting the Holy Spirit and proving yourselves ungrateful for his grace."

Bernard's way of life

At that time there was in that most luminous and love-filled valley a school of spiritual studies under Abbot Bernard. Here was to be found the fervor of regular discipline. He did everything and ordered everything to build a tabernacle for God on earth, according to the exemplar which had been shown to him on the mountain when he dwelt with God in the cloud in the solitude of Citeaux. After the first stages in his monastic life he became used to living in the company of ordinary men, and he learned to consider the weak and feeble by sympathizing with their weaknesses. How we longed for him to look after himself in the same way he looked after others — with as much gentleness, understanding and concern. But as soon as the year in which he was bound by obedience to Bishop William was ended, he went back to his former mode of life, just as a bowstring goes back to its tension when the archer fits the arrow or as rushing water cascades along its course after it has been damned up. It almost seemed as if he were trying to punish himself for being so idle for a long time or to penalize himself for neglecting to do the work belonging to the office of abbot.

Had you been there you would have seen a weak and feeble man making an attempt to carry out whatever he set his mind to, without a thought of whether he had the strength to do it. For others he was full of tenderness and care but paid no attention to his own well-being. He was a model of obedience in all things but would not listen to anyone who as a loving friend or as a superior told him to take heed for his own welfare. Taking no account of what he had done in the past, he had no mercy on his body when spurring himself to greater deeds. This increased striving after perfection, which involved further fasts and ceaseless vigils, gradually wore down that body already weakened through illness. . . .

Who in our days, be he ever so fit and strong, has ever done such wonderful deeds on behalf of the Church and for the glory of God as Bernard did and still does, in spite of his bad health bringing him to death's door? It would be hard to number the men whom by his word and example he attracted from the world and its ways not only to a new life but even to perfection. The whole Christian world is dotted with houses—or should I say cities—of refuge to which men may flee and be saved after falling into deadly sins worthy of eternal damnation, realizing their guilt and turning to the Lord. Think of how many churches he saved from falling into schism, how many heresies he routed. Who can remember how often he calmed the troubles caused by nations and churches, which threatened to break away from legitimate authority? But it is common knowledge that he did these things. How could one list the great benefits and helps he bestowed on individuals for all sorts of causes on behalf of so many different persons in different places and times?

Even if one finds fault with Bernard for allowing his zeal to overstep his limits, one must remember that godly souls respect that excess of his and, being themselves moved by the Spirit of God, they are very slow to blame him for it. Most of them excuse this so-called fault easily, since there are few who are so bold as to condemn a man whom God vindicates by doing so many marvelous things in him and through him. That man is happy indeed who is judged guilty of fault by doing something that most people do for the sake of boasting and self-glory. A youth such as he led would have been mistrusted in an ordinary young man, but he is truly blessed who fears the Lord always. He strove to increase by his own efforts the fullness of virtue with which grace had endowed him. But yet, that life of his, which was held up to others as a model to be imitated, could not possibly have lacked the example of frugal self-control. In this respect, even if he did carry things a little too far, he left to devout souls not so much an example of excess but rather an object lesson in fervor and zeal. And yet, why do we look for excuses for him about a thing for which he even to this day is ready to accuse himself? For everyone knows how afraid and suspicious he is of his own deeds and how he accuses himself of sacrilege because of his indiscreet zeal, which took his body away from the service of God and the brethren, instead of giving it to that service more thoroughly. But in spite of his sickness his strength returned and he became stronger, for the strength of God shines through his weakness, and even to this day men revere him more on this account. The fact that they revere him means that he has more authority, and that authority ensures a most thorough obedience on their part.

God's power shaped him for the great work of preaching. As you remember, he had been marked out for this work by a heavenly revelation while his mother was still carrying him in her womb. The whole development of his life trained him for this work, from the time he first went to Citeaux and lived there under obedience as a simple monk, until the time when he was made abbot of Clairvaux and ordained by William of Champeaux. This training in the monastery, although he could not foresee where it would lead him, prepared him for work not only on behalf of his own Order but also on behalf of the whole Church.

The first-fruits of his youth were dedicated to the work of restoring among his monks that fervor for the religious life which was found in the monks of Egypt long ago. He concentrated all his efforts by word and example to achieving this aim among the community in his monastery. But later, when his sickness forced him to adopt another way of life, as I have already told you, he could no longer play such an active part in the life of the monks. And this was how he was first forced into contact with men and women living in the world. They flocked to him in large numbers, and he had to adapt himself to their needs.

This was how he first came to preach the word of life abroad. The call of obedience drew him far away from his monastery to work in the Church's cause. Wherever he went and whenever he spoke, he was not silent about the things of God, nor would he cease to carry out God's work. And so it was that his reputation spread among men and women so widely that the Church could not afford not to use so valuable a member of Christ's body for its needs. From the very beginning, the Church has always been richly favored with the gifts of the Spirit. Now it was given full manifestation of the Spirit for what the apostle Paul calls the common good. Filled with faith he spoke with wisdom and knowledge, and his speaking was accompanied by the grace of prophecy and the working of miracles, including the healing of many diseases. I have heard of these things from men and women in whom I have trust and confidence.

. . .

Friendship enjoyed

I was unwell at Saint Thierry, drained of strength, and quite worn out by an illness that dragged on and on. When the man of God heard the news he sent his brother Gerard, of blessed memory, to bid me come to Clairvaux. He assured me that once there, I would speedily either regain my health or die. As for myself, seizing the opportunity God seemed to offer me of dying and in his company (which of the two then appealed to me more I really cannot say) I set out immediately and reached Clairvaux weary and in pain. The promise that had been made to me came true—the one I hoped at heart. My health was restored; by degrees my strength came back. Merciful God, what benefits that illness brought me—that rest, that freedom from every care. They satisfied some of my longing. Bernard's illness itself worked for my own good while I lay ill beside him. Flat on our backs, the two of us, we spent the livelong day talking about the spiritual nature of the soul and the cures which virtue furnishes for the illness of vice. It was then, so far as the length of my illness allowed, that he expounded on the Song of Songs for me, though only in the moral sense, without launching upon the mysteries with which the book abounds. This was what I had hoped for, what I had asked him to do. Every day, for fear of forgetting the things I had heard, I put them down insofar as God enabled me to and my memory served me. Thus I shared the insights of the man of God. As good-natured and disinterested as you please, he disclosed his ideas to me as they came to mind, and the meanings that his experience enabled him to make out. He outdid himself enlightening my utter ignorance of things that can only be known from personal experience. I could not as yet grasp all that he told me. But listening to him I realized as never before how far above me those lofty truths still soared. Enough said on that subject.

Chronology

Note: William's works and many of the events of his life cannot be
dated with certainty. The dates given here are those the editor judges
most probable.

1085   William was born in northern France.

1098   Robert of Molesme with his prior Alberic, subprior
Stephen and nineteen others found Citeaux, March
21.
William enters the Benedictine Abbey of Saint Nicaise at Rhiems with his brother, Simon.

1112   Bernard enters Citeaux with thirty relatives and
friends.

1115   Bernard founds Clairvaux with twelve other monks.

1118   Bernard is isolated from the community for a year.

1119   William visits Bernard at Clairvaux.
William is elected Abbot of Saint Thierry.

1121   William publishes his first work, *On Contemplating
God*.

1122   William writes *The Nature and Dignity of Love*.

1123   William recuperates at Clairvaux with Bernard. He writes *A Brief Commentary on the Song of Songs*.

1124   William seeks to resign as abbot and go to Clairvaux, but Bernard forbids it.

1125   Bernard writes his *Apologia* for William of St. Thierry.

1126   William writes his two-volume work *On the Nature of the Body and the Soul*.

1128   William writes *Exposition on the Letter to the Romans*. Bernard writes *On Grace and Free Will* for William of St. Thierry.

1129   William writes *On the Sacrament of the Altar*, which he dedicates to Bernard.

1130   William works on the *Commentaries on the Song of Songs*, drawn from the works of St. Gregory and St. Ambrose.

1131   William plays a leading role in the Chapter of Rheims to initiate reform among the Benedictines.

1135   William resigns as abbot of Saint Thierry and joins the Cistercian community at Signy.

1136   William puts together his *Meditations*.

1137   William begins his *Exposition on the Song of Songs*.

1138   William writes his *Disputation against Abelard* and stirs up Bernard to join the fray. To help the young, William prepares a trilogy: *Sentences on Faith, Mirror of Faith, Enigma of Faith*.

1143   William visits the Carthusians at Mont Dieu and returns home to write for them his *Golden Epistle*.

1145   William begins work on the *Life of Saint Bernard*.

1148   On September 8th, celebrated as the birthday of Blessed Mary, William dies peacefully at Signy.

1215   William's remains are moved from their tomb in the cloister to the church, signifying his beatification.

Select Bibliography

Note: A longer English Language Bibliography, up to 1983, can be found in M. Basil Pennington, *The Last of the Fathers,* pp. 172-180.

William of Saint Thierry. *The Works of William of Saint Thierry*, tr. Sister Penelope et. al., Cistercian Fathers Series (Spencer MA - Kalamazoo MI: Cistercian Publications, 1970—).

> *On Contemplating God, Prayer, Meditations*, vol. 1, CF 3 (1970)
> *Exposition on the Song of Songs*, vol. 2, CF 6 (1970)
> *The Enigma of Faith*, vol. 3, CF 9 (1974)
> *The Golden Epistle*, vol. 4, CF 12 (1971)
> *The Mirror of Faith*, vol. 5, CF 15 (1979)
> *Exposition on the Epistle to the Romans*, vol. 6, CF 27 (1980)
> *The Nature and Dignity of Love*, vol. 7, CF 30 (1981)

_____. "The Nature of the Body and Soul" tr. Benjamin Clark, in *Three Treatises on Man*, ed. Bernard McGinn, Cistercian Fathers Series, vol. 24 (Kalamazoo MI: Cistercian Publications, 1977), pp. 101-52.

_____. *St. Bernard of Clairvaux*, tr. Geoffrey Webb and Adrian Walker (Westminster MD: Newman, 1960).

Bell, David. *The Image and Likeness. The Augustinian Spirituality of William of St. Thierry*, Cistercian Studies Series 78 (Kalamazoo MI: Cistercian Publications, 1984).

_____. "The *Vita Antiqua* of William of St. Thierry" in *Cistercian Studies* 11 (1976) 246-55.

Bernard of Clairvaux. *The Works of Bernard of Clairvaux*, tr. Michael Casey et. al. (Spencer MA - Kalamazoo MI: Cistercian Publications, 1969—).

_____. *The Letters of St. Bernard of Clairvaux*, tr. Bruno Scott James (London: Burns and Oates, 1953).

Brooke, Odo, *Studies in Monastic Theology*, Cistercian Studies Series 37 (Kalamazoo MI: Cistercian Publications, 1980).

Bur, Michael, ed. *William, Abbot of Saint Thierry. A Colloquium at the Abbey of St. Thierry*, tr. Jerry Carfantan, Cistercian Studies Series 94 (Kalamazoo MI: Cistercian Publications, 1987).

Elder, E. Rozanne, ed. *The Spirituality of Western Christendom,* Cistercian Studies Series 30 (Kalamazoo MI: Cistercian Publications, 1976).

Fiske, Adele, "William of St. and Friendship" in *Citeaux* 12 (1961) 5-27.

Gilson, Etienne. *The Mystical Theology of Saint Bernard*, tr. A. H. C. Downes (Kalamazoo MI: Cistercian Publications, 1990).

Pennington, M. Basil. *The Last of the Fathers. The Cistercian Fathers of the Twelfth Century* (Still River MA: St. Bede's, 1983).

_____. ed. *One Yet Two. Monastic Tradition East and West* Cistercian Studies Series 29 (Kalamazoo MI: Cistercian Publications, 1976).

Savary, Louis, *Psychological Themes in the Golden Epistle of William of St. Thierry to the Carthusian of Mont Dieu, Analecta Cartusiana* 8 (Salzburg: Hogg, 1973).

Saward, Anne. "Man as the Image of God in the Works of William of St. Thierry" in *Cistercian Studies* 8 (1973) 309-36.

Summerfeldt, John R., ed., *Cistercian Ideals and Reality*, Cistercian Studies Series 60 (Kalamazoo MI: Cistercian Publications, 1978).

Thomas, Robert, "William of St. Thierry: Our Life in the Trinity" in *Monastic Studies* 3 (1965) 139-63.